The Self-Regulated Learning Guide

The Self-Regulated Learning Guide introduces K-12 teachers to the basics of self-regulation. Highly practical and supported by cutting-edge research, this book offers a variety of techniques for seamlessly infusing self-regulated learning principles into the classroom and for nurturing students' motivation to strategize, reflect, and succeed. Featuring clear explanations of the psychology of self-regulation, these nine chapters provide teachers with core concepts, realistic case scenarios, reflection activities, and more to apply SRL concepts to classroom activities with confidence.

Timothy J. Cleary is Associate Professor in the Department of School Psychology at Rutgers University, USA.

The Self-Regulated Learning Guide

Teaching Students to Think in the Language of Strategies

Timothy J. Cleary

Routledge
Taylor & Francis Group

NEW YORK AND LONDON

First published 2018
by Routledge
711 Third Avenue, New York, NY 10017

and by Routledge
2 Park Square, Milton Park, Abingdon, Oxon, OX14 4RN

Routledge is an imprint of the Taylor & Francis Group, an informa business

© 2018 Taylor & Francis

The right of Timothy J. Cleary to be identified as author of this work has been asserted by him in accordance with sections 77 and 78 of the Copyright, Designs and Patents Act 1988.

All rights reserved. No part of this book may be reprinted or reproduced or utilised in any form or by any electronic, mechanical, or other means, now known or hereafter invented, including photocopying and recording, or in any information storage or retrieval system, without permission in writing from the publishers.

Trademark notice: Product or corporate names may be trademarks or registered trademarks, and are used only for identification and explanation without intent to infringe.

Library of Congress Cataloging-in-Publication Data

Names: Cleary, Timothy J., author.
Title: The self-regulated learning guide : teaching students to think in the
   language of strategies/Timothy J. Cleary.
Description: New York : Routledge, 2018.
Identifiers: LCCN 2017030671 (print) | LCCN 2017038497 (ebook) |
   ISBN 9781315693378 (e-book) | ISBN 9781138910546 (hardback) |
   ISBN 9781138910553 (paperback) | ISBN 9781315693378 (ebook)
Subjects: LCSH: Learning strategies—Handbooks, manuals, etc.
Classification: LCC LB1066 (ebook) | LCC LB1066. C54 2018 (print) |
   DDC 370.15/23—dc23
LC record available at https://lccn.loc.gov/2017030671

ISBN: 978-1-138-91054-6 (hbk)
ISBN: 978-1-138-91055-3 (pbk)
ISBN: 978-1-315-69337-8 (ebk)

Typeset in Utopia
by Apex CoVantage, LLC

To all the teachers who have dedicated their careers to improving the lives of children. Your commitment and passion serve as a beacon of inspiration and hope for so many.

Contents

Meet the Author   *ix*
Acknowledgements   *xi*

Introduction   *1*

SECTION I   Preparing for Your SRL Journey   *5*

1 SRL LOOP: The Conceptual Foundation   *7*

2 Motivation: Fueling the SRL Loop   *19*

3 Strategies: Tools for Directing the SRL Loop   *37*

SECTION II   Digging a Little Bit Deeper   *51*

4 Forethought: Setting the Stage for Learning   *53*

5 Feedback: The Role of the Teacher   *71*

6 Feedback: Shifting Responsibility to the Student   *87*

7 Self-Reflection: Making Sense of Feedback   *101*

SECTION III   Bringing It All Together   *119*

8 Teaching SRL Skills: Classroom Testing Activities   *121*

9 Teaching SRL Skills: Classroom-Based Lessons and Activities   *139*

    Final Thoughts   *153*

Index   *155*

Meet the Author

Dr. Timothy J. Cleary is an Associate Professor in the Department of School Psychology in the Graduate School of Applied and Professional Psychology (GSAPP) at Rutgers University, USA. His primary research interests include the development and application of self-regulated learning (SRL) assessment and intervention practices across academic, athletic, and clinical contexts. Dr. Cleary has published over 40 peer-reviewed journal articles and book chapters along with two edited books, specifically addressing SRL topics and applications. Dr. Cleary teaches courses in academic assessments and interventions, learning disabilities, and SRL practices, and provides professional development workshops to teachers and administrators in K-12 and college contexts. He also actively consults with educators and scholars around the world regarding the application of SRL principles.

Acknowledgements ● ● ● ● ●

Many personal milestones and achievements are a function of the support and guidance that one receives from others. The publishing of this book was no exception.

To my parents … for instilling a sense of self-discipline and self-regulation during my childhood.

To Professor Zimmerman … a mentor and friend who gently laid the foundation for my professional pathway and career.

To my SRL colleagues and friends … you have all shaped and guided my thinking about SRL principles and applications to real-world contexts.

To my current and former graduate students … my understanding of SRL continually deepens from your insights and contributions to our research projects.

To Caroline Gergel, Katie Zimmerman, and Heather Bryer … your comments and feedback on earlier versions of this book were incredibly helpful.

To my family, my wife, Deborah, and my two boys, Benjamin and Maximillian … your presence in my life inspires me to become the best person that I can be.

Introduction ●●●●●

I believe with all my heart that the American classroom teachers are one of our greatest and most heroic treasures.

—Patricia Polacco

Teaching represents one of the most underappreciated yet influential professions in our society. As Patricia Polacco noted, many teachers are viewed as heroes – that is, people who do courageous things or who act in noble or magnanimous ways. Although people may define a "hero teacher" in different ways, I have typically admired those who are able to effortlessly cultivate warm and supportive classroom environments while simultaneously dealing with the complex and overwhelming aspects of being a teacher.

In addition to dealing with typical classroom management issues, class prep work, and grading, teachers must be able to flexibly adapt to changing policy and curriculum initiatives, such as No Child Left Behind, Common Core standards, or Next Generation Science Standards. To keep up with these changes, teachers are asked to attend professional development workshops and then incorporate these new ideas (often immediately) into their teaching. When one also considers the burden that school-wide standardized testing and unanticipated disruptions (e.g., school closings) place on available instructional time, teachers are often forced to come up with creative ways to adequately address the curriculum.

Along a similar vein, it is frustrating for many teachers because of the constant barrage of messages they receive from administrators, researchers, and policy makers about *what* and *how* they need to teach. To be honest, I was nervous when first deciding to write this book because I thought I would be viewed as just one more person in this long tradition of telling teachers what they need to do. If I were you, I would probably approach this book with some degree of skepticism and caution, asking myself, *"What 'extra' things will the author be telling me I need to add to my instruction?"*, *"Isn't SRL similar to other things that we already do in the classroom?"*, or perhaps even, *"Is SRL just another fad or another short-term trend in education?"* From my perspective, all of these questions are legitimate and fair.

To address these concerns, let me start by stating that SRL instruction is certainly not a fad or a superficial "hot topic." It is also not another "swing in the educational pendulum" that is so common in schools. The reality is that, regardless of age, skill level, gender, ethnicity, home environment, etc., all students will encounter situations that are challenging and difficult. That is, situations that require students to persevere and persist, to remain positive and resolute in the face of failure, and to adapt or change their behaviors when not performing successfully – a set of skills that collectively embodies the term *self-regulated learning (SRL)*.

In this book, I do not tell you things that you "must" or "have to" do in order to become an effective teacher of SRL skills. I am confident that most of you are all well-trained teachers who know more about teaching K-12 students than I do. What I am attempting to do in this book, however, is to flesh out the meaning of SRL and to offer some tips and recommendations regarding how you can directly infuse SRL ideas and principles into your classroom lessons and activities.

Another unique aspect of engaging in SRL instruction is that it will naturally lead you to think about yourself and your teaching in new and enriching ways. Thus, as you read about different SRL processes and skills, you will likely question your prior conceptions and beliefs about student learning and capabilities, or perhaps the ways in which you provide feedback or interact with students. As you begin to apply SRL to your teaching, you will also notice that it does not take up a lot of your time. In fact, when implemented in an adaptive way, SRL principles become a natural part of the fabric and routines of typical classroom instructional activities.

As a final point, although helping your students regulate more effectively will certainly benefit them in many ways, it does not guarantee their success in school. Thus, SRL instruction should not be viewed as a type of panacea or silver bullet. Even if you implement to perfection every SRL and motivation principle that I recommend in this book, you will still likely encounter students who are not motivated to learn, who exhibit weak academic skills, and who exhibit inconsistent homework completion. However, from my perspective you will greatly increase the odds of your students becoming more self-reliant, motivated, and successful if you are able to nurture and enhance their SRL skills.

●●●●●

Purposes of this Book

In a simplistic sense, this book is about you and your role as a K-12 teacher. The book is designed to help you develop a solid understanding of SRL principles and the various methods for applying and extending these principles into classroom contexts. Throughout this book, you will be prompted to openly and honestly reflect on the quality of the activities you assign students and the nature of your feedback and interactions with students. It is my hope that by the end of the book you will recognize that SRL instruction and your traditional instructional approach are not separate or distinct; rather, they complement, inform, and influence each other.

For many of you, this book represents the *start* of a journey towards becoming an SRL guide or facilitator. Although I am fairly confident that you will learn many things, it is important to recognize that you will not become an SRL expert by simply reading this book. Becoming proficient in anything requires practice and refinement. Thus, take your time and be gentle with yourself as you attempt to apply SRL in your classroom. Ask others for feedback, circle back and re-read sections or parts of this book, and/or seek out SRL professional development opportunities to refine these skills. Most of all, have fun and be creative when thinking about how SRL fits with your teaching.

●●●●●

Organization of this Book

I organized this book into three sections: *Preparing for Your SRL Journey, Digging a Little Bit Deeper,* and *Bringing it All Together.* These three sections depict a phase-based approach to teaching SRL that begins with an introduction to core SRL principles (Section I), followed by an exploration of how essential SRL processes can be infused into classrooms (Section II), and then an illustration of how teachers can integrate multiple SRL themes during authentic classroom experiences (Section III). Because each section builds on and complements the prior one, I strongly encourage you to read the sections and chapters in sequence.

Section I Preparing for Your SRL Journey. The first phase of your SRL journey involves learning about the conceptual foundation of SRL. In Chapter 1, I define and explain the meaning of SRL while placing particular emphasis on the concept of a *cyclical feedback loop*. The next two chapters address two essential themes of the cyclical, regulatory process: *student motivation* (the will) and *strategic action* (the skill). Chapter 2 addresses five types of student beliefs (i.e., self-efficacy, interest, value, mindsets, autonomy) that can directly influence student effort, persistence, and resilience in the classroom. In Chapter 3, I shift the focus to the importance of strategic thinking and action as students learn. A central theme emphasized in this latter chapter (and actually throughout the entire book) involves getting students to THINK IN THE LANGUAGE OF STRATEGIES.

Section II Digging a Little Bit Deeper. In the next phase of your journey, I unpack the SRL cyclical feedback loop to reveal its component parts and processes. It is within Section II that I address how you can teach specific SRL skills to your students, such as goal-setting and task analysis (Chapter 4), self-monitoring (Chapter 6), and self-reflection (Chapter 7). I also discuss the importance of your feedback messages and how these messages can either facilitate or undermine student motivation to self-regulate (Chapter 5). Collectively, Section II chapters are designed to bring the SRL cyclical feedback loop to life by conveying the process through which students approach, complete, and refine their performance on classroom activities.

Section III Bringing it All Together. The first two sections of this book introduce you to SRL principles as well as innovative techniques for infusing those principles in your classroom. What is missing, however, is an illustration of how you can integrate these principles and ideas in an authentic and holistic fashion. In the *Bringing it All Together* phase of your SRL journey, I provide a snapshot of how you can integrate multiple SRL processes (goals, planning, monitoring, attributions, etc.) in your instruction and interactions with students. I discuss this integrative SRL instructional approach with respect to test preparation and test review activities (Chapter 8), and classroom-based assignments or projects (Chapter 9). It is my hope that after reading these final two chapters, you will have gained new insights into the thought processes and reasoning behind the development and implementation of SRL innovations.

⬤ ⬤ ⬤ ⬤ ⬤

Approach and Special Features

When writing this book, I wanted to discuss SRL concepts using a conversational tone that minimizes technical jargon and theory. I also wanted to write a book that was accessible and directly relevant to your role as a teacher. To this end, I framed many of my descriptions and case scenarios in relation to specific learning activities, assignments, or projects that teachers often assign students. I also continuously prompt you to think about all SRL principles and ideas in relation to the activities that you emphasize in your classes. It is my hope that you will be able to more easily apply SRL concepts after you have thought about how SRL is naturally linked with classroom-based activities.

To further enhance the authenticity and relevance of this book, I included several supplemental features in each chapter. I briefly summarize the purpose and aspects of these features below.

Quote. Each chapter begins with a quote from a notable author, sports figure, educational activist, or historical figure. I selected each particular quote because it focuses on an issue, idea, or concept embedded within a given chapter.

Chapter Snapshot. The Chapter Snapshot feature presents a brief description of the objectives and scope of the chapter. It provides a concise yet broad overview of core ideas.

Reader Reflection. The Reader Reflection exercises are presented at the outset of each chapter to stimulate your thinking about a core issue or theme addressed in the chapter. This feature should prime your thinking and get you ready to tackle the target SRL concepts.

Reflect and Connect. In most chapters, I present two or three Reflect and Connect exercises. These exercises represent a type of "check-in" activity, whereby you are prompted to think about an SRL principle mentioned in the chapter relative to your particular teaching approaches or classroom experiences.

Core Concepts. In all chapters, I present several brief, take-away themes. These messages represent tidbits or "golden nuggets" regarding an SRL principle, an instructional approach, or recommendation for incorporating SRL in the classroom.

Tales of the Student. I present several Tales of the Student throughout the book. These hypothetical case vignettes convey the regulatory thoughts, behaviors, and emotions exhibited by students as they attempt to learn in a given content area. Although many students are presented, the four main student characters include *Tanya* (5th grade), *Michael* (7th grade), *Peter* (9th grade), and *Johanna* (11th grade). By including students who differ in grade level, achievement status, and motivational and SRL profile, you will have an opportunity to see SRL processes unfold and manifest across different individuals in various situations and contexts.

Tales of the Teacher. I use the Tales of the Teacher feature to convey teacher perceptions and instructional practices. Although I present many hypothetical teacher case scenarios, I emphasize teachers who were connected to the four main student characters: *Ms. Martinez* (5th grade teacher – Tanya), *Mr. Jones* (7th grade English Language Arts teacher – Michael), *Ms. Johnson* (9th grade science teacher – Peter), and *Mr. Filipo* (11th grade physics teacher – Johanna).

Conversations with ... At several points throughout the book, I provide a dialogue between teachers and different individuals: students, other teachers, and principals. These conversations are designed to illustrate the challenges, thought processes, and reasoning underlying teachers' attempts to infuse SRL ideas into the classroom.

Figures and Tables. The final features include tables and figures. These features are used to clarify, summarize, and/or elaborate on SRL principles and concepts presented in the text.

Section I

Preparing for Your SRL Journey

1

SRL LOOP: The Conceptual Foundation

The ultimate measure of a man is not where he stands in moments of comfort and convenience, but where he stands at times of challenge and controversy.

—Dr. Martin Luther King

 Chapter Snapshot

In this book, I take you on a journey of discovery and reflection about self-regulated learning (SRL) and its application to classroom contexts. To get started, I would like to focus on theory (just a little, I promise!) and a few overarching principles of SRL. Although this chapter can get a bit "dry" at times, it is one of the most important because it introduces several core SRL themes emphasized throughout the book:

- the role of "challenge" and SRL in students' learning experiences
- essential characteristics of self-regulated learners (SRLers)
- SRL as a cyclical feedback loop.

So let's get started and have you begin your SRL journey.

Reader Reflection – 1.1 The Nature of a Challenge

At the beginning of most chapters in this book, I will ask you to reflect on your teaching or personal experiences that relate to SRL principles. For this chapter, I would like you to answer the following two questions:

- What are the top two to three "challenges" that your students typically encounter in your courses? In other words, what things are hard for them as they attempt to complete assignments, tests, or projects?

- Do you do anything specific to help them overcome these challenges? Like what?

Challenges are Inevitable

A challenge can be defined as a difficult task, a problem, or something that is hard for people to do. It often involves a mismatch between students' thinking, knowledge, or skills and the demands and expectations of a situation or activity. A challenge can also vary in scope or complexity, such as completing a five-problem mathematics worksheet versus designing and completing a physics experiment.

An interesting aspect of challenges, however, is that they are often subjective in nature. For example, whereas some students may identify studying and remembering course content as a primary area of difficulty, others may believe that writing essays or completing science lab reports are the key obstacles to overcome. Along a similar vein, students on the Honor Roll may believe that increasing their course grades from an A- to an A is a daunting challenge, whereas lower-achieving students may view getting a B in mathematics as major cause for celebration. Simply put, a challenge is often in the eye of the beholder.

Despite these differences in perception, most students are likely to view situations as challenging when the "rules of the game" change. Consider the experience of transitioning from elementary to middle school. In elementary schools, teachers tend to assume the role of an *executive control commander*– someone who directs the ship and who provides extensive instruction, assistance, and guidance regarding when, how, and why students need to do certain things. Upon entering middle school, however, things begin to change (Grolnick & Raftery-Helmer, 2015). Students are exposed to a more intensive curriculum and must learn to deal with a diverse set of requirements, rules, and demands from a "team" of teachers. They also face increased expectations for self-sufficiency and independence, in part because most assignments are designed to be completed outside of the classroom (e.g., long-term research papers, studying for unit exams). A similar game-changing situation occurs when students transition to high school, go off to college and/or graduate school, and/or enter the workforce. Each of these transitions represent a defining moment for students in that they must figure out *what* and *how* they need to adapt or change in order to meet new expectations.

As a teacher, you are on the front lines with students. You get to witness how students cope with and react to these challenging moments. To explore your thoughts about challenging experiences in your classroom, please complete Reflect and Connect exercise 1.1.

Reflect and Connect – 1.1 Challenges in School

Take a minute to think about the students in your classroom and the challenges that many of them face.

- Do you ever speak to your students about these challenges? What are these conversations like?

  _____

  _____

- From your experience, are most students able to overcome their learning difficulties?

  _____

  _____

Paralleling Dr. Martin Luther King's quote presented at the outset of the chapter, it is important for administrators, teachers, and parents to recognize that all students will naturally encounter challenges or "bumps in the road" as they progress through school – it is simply inevitable. When you throw into the mix that these bumps often co-exist with negative emotions (e.g., anxiety, depression, and anger) and social difficulties (Suveg, Davis, & Jones, 2015), it is easy to understand why many students disengage, avoid, and dislike school.

From my perspective, however, challenges are not necessarily a bad thing. They are not things to avoid. Rather, when viewed from a strength-based or growth perspective, challenges represent a potential stepping-stone or an opportunity for students to develop and grow as learners. In this book, I promote the premise that students can transform difficult learning circumstances into successes when they are able to:

- recognize when they are encountering a challenge
- understand the nature and characteristics of that challenge
- display the desire or will to deal with the challenge
- develop effective strategic plans to overcome the challenge
- evaluate their progress in overcoming the challenge.

In short, students will most likely overcome challenges when they exhibit strong *self-regulated learning (SRL) skills*.

> **Core Concept 1.1**
>
> Encountering challenge is a necessary part of learning and growth. You can help students confront and overcome challenges by nurturing their SRL skills and motivation.

Portrait of a Self-Regulated Learner (SRLer)

On several occasions, teachers have asked me, "What exactly is SRL?" or "What types of things would I see a self-regulated learner (SRLer) do?" SRL is a concept that, while complex and nuanced, is also fairly simple and intuitive to understand. At a theoretical or conceptual level, SRLers are those who exhibit behaviors or patterns of thinking characterized by adaptive *motivation* (students' willingness or desire to engage in learning and to display effort and persistence), high quality *strategic action* (students' purposeful, intentional use of tactics and procedures to learn), and strong *metacognitive knowledge and skills* (students' self-awareness and knowledge of learning activities along with their attempts to plan, monitor, and evaluate; Butler, Schnellert, & Perry, 2017; Cleary, 2015). More simply, SRLers are those who want to perform well on some activity and who purposefully and strategically figure out ways to achieve their goals (see Table 1.1).

The above description of SRLers parallels what experts in many fields describe as highly accomplished and successful individuals. Bill Parcells, a Hall of Fame NFL football coach, describes highly successful individuals as those who *find a way to win* (Parcells, 1995). From his viewpoint, success is not simply the result of mere desire or motivation to excel – it involves the effective use of resources and tools to achieve one's goals. In this book, I adhere to a similar expression that underscores the heart and essence of SRLers – that is, individuals who, despite experiencing challenges, barriers,

Table 1.1 Core characteristics of SRLers

- **Self-starter** – takes initiative; does not need to be told multiple times to do something
- **Proactive** – anticipates and prepares ahead to deal with a challenge
- **Goal-directed** – selects specific things to attain or accomplish
- **Planning-oriented** – decides on a course of action to accomplish goals
- **Strategic** – uses tactics and specific methods to enhance learning
- **Self-aware** – mindful about strengths and weaknesses
- **Self-reflective** – evaluates performance and the potential causes of performance
- **Adaptive and flexible** – adjusts behaviors and strategies as needed

or struggles, continuously *find a way to learn* (see Tales of the Student – 1.1). Three core concepts typically subsume the characteristics of an SRLer: motivation, strategic thinking and action, and metacognition.

Tales of the Student – 1.1 Michael

Michael, a 7th grade student in a middle school, is a hard-working student. Although Michael does not perform at the top of his class in terms of grades (he typically earns B grades in most classes), he is very responsible and completes all of his classwork and homework assignments on time. Further, despite his occasional struggle on an exam or assignment, Michael does not seem to become too upset about his grades. He possesses a quiet confidence about himself and understands that mistakes are a natural part of the learning process. His teachers have been amazed at all of the positive things that Michael says to himself, even when struggling, such as "You will do better next time. Just keep practicing." Michael is also quite strategic as he learns. That is, he thinks about the best approach to studying or writing an essay and is particularly interested in figuring out the most efficient ways of doing things.

What makes Michael fairly unique compared to most kids his age, however, is how well he thinks ahead and reflects on his performance in school. Michael plans how he will study before most tests and constantly thinks about the things he can do better in order to increase his grades. Michael also keeps track of things that are difficult for him at home, which prompts him to seek out help and assistance from his teachers. Finally, when provided with feedback or grades on an assignment, Michael devotes some time to analyze his performance and to reflect on the things that he might need to do differently to improve on the next assignment.

Motivation

At a core level, SRLers are *highly motivated*. Like Michael, SRLers try hard in school and will often persevere when challenged. They do not need to be reminded or prodded to do their work; they take the initiative and purposefully strive to regulate or manage their thoughts, actions, or their learning environments to get things done. In many cases, the internal spark for self-motivation is a function of the types of beliefs, perceptions, and mindsets that students possess as well as their commitment to attaining their goals (Schunk & Zimmerman, 2008; see Chapter 2).

Strategic Thinking and Action

Exhibiting motivated and goal-directed behaviors is only one variable in the equation of success. Like Michael, SRLers are very *strategic* in their thinking and approach to learning. They have a toolbox or repertoire of *learning strategies* from which to choose when learning course content or while engaged in reading, writing, and mathematics activities (Weinstein & Palmer, 2002). SRLers also utilize strategies to control their thoughts, emotions, and environments when learning, such as Michael making positive self-statements when frustrated or arranging a quiet place to study at home (Wolters, 2011).

Metacognitive Skills

SRLers also exhibit strong metacognition skills – various ways of thinking about their own thinking. They plan and think ahead and continuously evaluate how they perform. Although they are not always consciously aware of their behaviors during learning, they tend to notice when learning goes awry or when their strategies are not working. Similar to Michael, SRLers tend to track their learning progress and are mindful of the specific challenges or mistakes that they make during learning. Conversely, students who regulate less effectively often lack insight about their thinking and behaviors due to poor monitoring skills (see Tales of the Student – 1.2).

Tales of the Student – 1.2 Tanya

Tanya is a 5th grade student who has struggled over the past couple of years in elementary school. Standardized state testing revealed a somewhat consistent profile of age-appropriate academic skills, although some of her skills are slightly below average. Math and science are particularly difficult for Tanya as she fails many tests and finds some of the concepts to be too abstract and confusing. Tanya has a set way to study, which at best consists of using index cards and reading over her notes or study guides. To make matters worse, Tanya has developed a sense of helplessness about school because she does not really understand why things are so difficult. Her teacher also expressed concerns about Tanya's inconsistent homework completion, her tendency to give up easily, and her overall negative attitudes about school. Tanya's parents are frustrated because they believe that although Tanya possesses the capacity to perform better, she does not "consistently apply herself." Tanya does not reveal it to her parents or teachers, but she truly wants to do better in school – she is just at a loss for how to accomplish this.

SRL: A Set of Characteristics or a Cyclical Process?

When I provide professional development workshops or speak to teachers about SRL, I first describe the core behaviors and characteristics that SRLers might exhibit in the classroom (see previous section and Table 1.1). This type of "descriptive analysis" is useful because it enables teachers to conjure up images of students who fit the mold of an SRLer. Many of them find this explanation of SRL exciting, but they quickly feel dissatisfied because they want to know more. Specifically, they want to learn about *how* they can develop SRL skills in their students.

It is at this moment when I shift the conversation from a focus on "**characteristics** of SRL" to the "***process*** of SRL." This change in focus is essential given that most contemporary theorists define SRL as a process – a coordinated set of actions and beliefs that are planned, implemented, and adapted as needed to accomplish or attain a goal

(Efklides, 2011; Winne & Hadwin, 1998; Zimmerman, 2000). That is, it is a process through which individuals approach and complete a learning activity, and then make judgments about how they need to improve in the future.

When shifting to a process focus of SRL, I typically ask teachers, *"Why is it important to focus on SRL as a process rather than as a set of specific behaviors or skills?"* Through our discussion, we hit upon a couple of important ideas. First, a process account of SRL does not simply describe what regulated behaviors should look like. It emphasizes the ways in which students go about managing their learning – their approach, use of strategies, ways of thinking, and reflecting, etc. By adopting a process SRL perspective, teachers have the potential to more effectively assess how students get off track and, more importantly, to develop ideas about strategies students need to use to improve.

A second important take-away theme is that process accounts of SRL integrate many different variables and constructs to explain *how* and *why* students regulate. Thus, they depict SRL in a coherent and conceptual way so that one can identify how the different aspects of SRL – goals, plans, use of strategies, motivation, and self-reflection – operate in concert to explain performance. When teachers understand the how and why of students' learning behaviors, they are more likely to sufficiently address an age-old question for teachers, *"How can I help my students learn and perform at an optimal level?"*

Core Concept 1.2

Viewing SRL as a cyclical, multi-phase *process* of thinking and action can help you understand the specific beliefs, behaviors, or skills that students need to adapt or improve.

A Three-Phase Model of SRL

Most contemporary theories depict the process of SRL in terms of a *cyclical feedback loop* (Cleary, 2015); a data-generation process through which individuals gather and use feedback about performance to self-evaluate and to improve. In this book, I emphasize Barry Zimmerman's (2000) version of the SRL feedback loop. This model includes three sequential and related phases: forethought, performance control, and self-reflection (see Figure 1.1). Zimmerman's feedback loop is emphasized because it integrates all of the core dimensions of SRL (i.e., motivation, strategic action, and metacognitive skills) and has been successfully applied to a wide range of fields, such as education, sports, and leisure (Bembenutty, Cleary, & Kitsantas, 2013). This model has also been lauded by educators and researchers as highly accessible and relevant to academic tasks.

Zimmerman (2000) defines SRL as "self-generated thoughts, feelings, and actions that are planned and cyclically adapted to the attainment of personal goals" (p. 14). Like most SRL theorists, he envisioned SRL as a process of thinking and action. The regulatory process begins with the *forethought phase*, which includes task analysis (goal-setting, planning) and motivational beliefs. These "pre-action" processes set the stage for learning by helping students understand what is being asked of them and what might be their best approach to learning (see Chapter 4). The extent to which SRLers think ahead or engage in forethought is important because it influences the

Figure 1.1 Phases and processes of self-regulation.
Source: From "Motivating self-regulated problem solvers" by B. J. Zimmerman & M. Campillo (2003). In J. E. Davidson & R. J. Sternberg (Eds.), *The psychology of problem solving* (p. 239). New York: Cambridge University Press. Reprinted with permission.

quality with which they strategically engage in the learning activity. This phase also considers the role that student beliefs and perceptions have on their desire to engage in the rest of the feedback loop (see Chapter 2).

As SRLers attempt to learn, often referred to as the *performance phase*, they utilize different *tactics* and *strategies* (see Chapter 3). SRLers often use various procedures to complete mathematics word problems (e.g., identify the problem, represent the problem as a picture, etc.), to self-motivate (e.g., give oneself a cookie or treat after studying for an hour), to manage their emotions (e.g., deep breathing, relaxation) or to structure their home study environments to optimize learning (e.g., quiet location). During learning, SRLers also *self-monitor* or keep track of their performance and the many challenges or obstacles they encounter (Chapter 6). As previously noted, Michael likes to keep track of things that confuse him when completing homework assignments or studying. By tracking these areas, Michael is able to remember the things he needs to ask his teachers during the next day of class. Self-monitored information, as well as feedback provided by teachers and others (see Chapter 5), is at the very heart or essence of the feedback loop. That is, for a feedback loop to operate effectively, students must have access to information that enables them to *reflect* on how things are progressing.

Similar to forethought and performance control, the *self-reflection* phase (see Chapter 7) involves many different processes. However, the function of self-reflection is to help students determine how well they performed (*self-evaluation*), the reasons why they performed that way (*attributions*), their affective reactions (*satisfaction, frustration*), and their decisions about how best to improve (*adaptive inferences*). Ultimately, the types of reflective judgments and reactions students exhibit have a major influence over how they approach future learning tasks.

In Chapters 2 to 7, I devote most of my attention to unpacking the three-phase cyclical model of SRL, and emphasize how teachers can apply these SRL principles to the classroom.

SRL LOOP: The Conceptual Foundation

Core Concept 1.3

The process of SRL involves a coordinated integration of distinct yet related sub-processes subsumed within the three-phase cyclical feedback loop (forethought, performance, self-reflection).

Linking SRL to School-Based Learning Activities

Reflect and Connect – 1.2 Learning Activities as a Process

Identify a learning activity (e.g., small group reading activity, science labs, class lectures) or performance outcome (e.g., tests, quizzes, projects) that is of central importance to your class.

- To what extent have you thought about this activity as a *process* with a before, during, and after dimension?

  _____

  _____

- As a teacher, does understanding this temporal dimension of a learning activity (i.e., before, during, and after) matter? Why or why not?

  _____

  _____

Before reading this section, please complete Reflect and Connect exercise 1.2. As you probably already know, teachers ask students to engage in a wide range of activities over the course of a school year, such as daily homework assignments, small group reading lessons, short-term and long-term projects, essay writing assignments, and test preparation or studying activities. In a sense, a major thrust of your job as a teacher is to develop relevant learning activities or assignments and then to evaluate your students' performance and competencies on these assignments. Although learning activities play a central role in all classrooms, what do they have to do with SRL and this book? This is a critical issue for me to address.

Research has shown that students' SRL skills and behaviors will often vary based on a given situation or context (Cleary & Chen, 2009; Winne & Jamieson-Noel, 2002). In addition, SRL instruction tends to be most effective when it is linked to a specific content area and/or to specific learning tasks within the given content area (Hattie & Donoghue, 2016). Thus, it is much more relevant and informative to examine how well students regulate as they prepare for mathematics exams or write essays assigned in their Language Arts class than it is to explore how they regulate in a more general or broad sense. Thus, as you learn about SRL themes and practices in this book, I encourage you to think about how your classroom assignments and projects fit or relate with these themes.

As part of Reflect and Connect exercise 1.2, I asked you to identify the before, during, and after dimensions of a core learning activity used in your class. How well were you able to do this? Have you ever thought about your learning activities in this way? Although I suspect some of you were able to describe your assignments in terms of this before, during, after sequence, for others this may have been more challenging. Regardless, it is important to recognize two important things as you strive to apply SRL in your classroom:

- the need to understand the demands and challenges of the learning activities you assign your students
- the need to identify the before, during, and after dimensions of these learning activities.

As you can see in Figure 1.2, the temporal dimensions of learning activities (before, during, and after) mirror the forethought, performance, and reflection phase processes of SRL. That is, certain SRL processes are well aligned with the *before* aspects of a learning activity (e.g., goals, planning), whereas other processes are linked to the *during* (e.g., strategies, self-monitoring) or *after* components (e.g., self-evaluation, attributions). Understanding this connection between task temporal dimensions and SRL phases will help guide your thinking about *which* SRL skills to emphasize during learning and *when* you should emphasize them.

Suppose Ms. Martinez gave Tanya and her classmates two days to complete a persuasive essay assignment in her Language Arts class. When viewing this activity from a process perspective, there is a *before* component (i.e., time before students begin to write the essay), a *during* component (i.e., when students actually write and complete the essay), and an *after* component (i.e., point at which students have received some type of performance feedback). In other words, Ms. Martinez wants Tanya and her classmates to think about and do certain things:

- as they *prepare* to write the essay
- *when writing* the essay
- *after* they have written the essay.

For example, before Tanya begins writing the essay it would be helpful if she organized the necessary materials, clarified the nature of the essay requirements, brainstormed ideas, or perhaps wrote an outline. In her attempts to write the essay, Tanya would likely benefit from using the persuasive essay strategies taught by Ms. Martinez and strategies for structuring a quiet place at home to write her essays. When she is involved in the actual drafting of the essay, it may also be helpful for Tanya to keep track of how well she used the strategies and whether certain aspects of the assignment

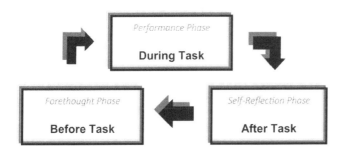

Figure 1.2 **Link between temporal dimensions of a learning activity and the three-phase SRL process**

are difficult for her. Upon receiving feedback or a grade from Ms. Martinez about the essay, Tanya should then attempt to engage in self-reflection (self-evaluation, attributions, adaptive inferences) to determine how well she performed and the things she might need to do differently to improve.

The Tanya scenario is a simple illustration of the link between the sequential process of a learning assignment and the SRL skills related to this process. Throughout this book, I repeatedly emphasize the things that you should think about and do to better align SRL principles to your learning activities. See Tales of the Teacher – 1.1 to further illustrate this point.

Tales of the Teacher – 1.1 Mr. Jones

As a natural part of writing instruction, Michael's English Language Arts teacher, Mr. Jones, has his class work in small groups of approximately three to four students. Within this small group context, he encourages students to talk about three important questions related to the forethought phase of SRL (see Chapter 4): (a) What are the key expectations and requirements of the writing assignment (task analysis)?; (b) What is your goal as you prepare to do this writing assignment (goal-setting)?; and (c) Do you have a plan on how you will approach this assignment (strategic planning)? As a part of this activity, all students are asked to write out their answers to the questions, share their responses with classmates, and then submit the forms to Mr. Jones at the end of class. Mr. Jones also walks around the room to listen for the types of regulatory processes that students exhibit. By obtaining a snapshot of information about how his students approach and think about the assigned activity and using a regulatory framework from which to understand their thinking and actions, Mr. Jones is in a much better position to provide feedback, advice, and remedial instruction to those students who need it.

Core Concept 1.4

To successfully apply SRL principles in your classroom, you first need to become knowledgeable of the core features of SRL concepts as well as the key characteristics of learning activities used in your classes.

Concluding Thoughts

The purpose of this chapter was to provide an overview of several key SRL principles and concepts that permeate this book. Regardless of the specific chapter that you are reading, it is important to keep the following guidelines in mind. You should strive to:

- develop a deep and nuanced understanding of the assignments and activities used in your classes
- identify the most common and intensive challenges your students encounter when completing these activities
- determine how the before, during, and after aspects of your learning activities link to the three-phase process of SRL
- teach students about SRL skills as they complete learning activities.

References

Bembenutty, H., Cleary, T. J., & Kitsantas, A. (Eds.). (2013). *Applications of self-regulated learning across diverse disciplines: A tribute to Barry J. Zimmerman*. Charlotte, NC: Information Age Publishing.

Butler, D. L., Schnellert, L., & Perry, N. E. (2017). *Developing self-regulating learners*. Upper Saddle River, NJ: Pearson Education, Inc.

Cleary, T. J. (2015). *Self-regulated learning interventions with at-risk youth: Enhancing adaptability, performance, and well-being*. Washington, DC: American Psychological Association.

Cleary, T. J., & Chen, P. P. (2009). Self-regulation, motivation, and math achievement in middle school: Variations across grade level and math context. *Journal of School Psychology, 47*(5), 291–314. doi:10.1016/j.jsp.2009.04.002.

Efklides, A. (2011). Interactions of metacognition with motivation and affect in self-regulated learning: The MASRL model. *Educational Psychologist, 46*(1), 6–25. doi:10.1080/00461520.2011.538645.

Grolnick, W. S., & Raftery-Helmer, J. N. (2015). Contexts supporting self-regulated learning at school transitions. In T. J. Cleary (Ed.), *Self-regulated learning interventions with at-risk youth: Enhancing adaptability, performance, and well-being* (pp. 251–276). Washington, DC: American Psychological Association.

Hattie, J. A. C., & Donoghue, G. M. (2016). Learning strategies: a synthesis and conceptual model. *Science of Learning. 1*, 16013. doi:10.1038/npjscilearn.2016.13.

Parcells, B. (1995). *Finding a way to win: The principles of leadership, teamwork, and motivation*. New York: Doubleday.

Schunk, D. H., & Zimmerman, B. J. (2008). *Motivation and self-regulated learning: Theory, research, and applications*. New York: Lawrence Erlbaum Associates.

Suveg, C., Davis, M., & Jones, A. (2015). Emotional regulation interventions for youth with anxiety disorders. In T. J. Cleary (Ed.), *Self-regulated learning interventions with at-risk youth: Enhancing adaptability, performance, and well-being* (pp. 137–156). Washington DC: American Psychological Association.

Weinstein, C. E., & Palmer, D. R. (2002). *User's manual for those administering the learning and study strategies inventory* (2nd ed.). Clearwater, FL: H & H Publishing.

Winne, P. H., & Jamieson-Noel, D. (2002). Exploring students' calibration of self reports about study tactics and achievement. *Contemporary Educational Psychology, 27*(4), 551–572. doi:10.1016/S0361-476X(02)00006-1.

Winne, P. H., & Hadwin, A. F. (1998). Studying as self-regulated learning. In D. Hacker, J. Dunlosky, & A. Graesser (Eds.), *Metacognition in educational theory and practice* (pp. 277–304). Hillsdale, NJ: Lawrence Erlbaum.

Wolters, C. A. (2011). Regulation of motivation: Contextual and social aspects. *Teacher College Record, 113*, 265–283.

Zimmerman, B. J. (2000). Attaining self-regulation: A social cognitive perspective. In M. Boekaerts, P. Pintrich, & M. Zeidner (Eds.), *Self-regulation: Theory, research, and applications* (pp. 13–39). Orlando, FL: Academic Press.

2

Motivation: Fueling the SRL Loop

We expert teachers know that motivation and emotional impact are what matter.
—Donald Norman

 Chapter Snapshot

In Chapter 2, I discuss an aspect of SRL that tends to be of great interest to most teachers – *student motivation*. In addition to providing an overview of motivation and its importance in school contexts, I focus on five types of motivation beliefs (i.e., self-efficacy beliefs, interest, value or instrumentality, autonomy, and growth mindset) shown to predict students' academic behaviors and achievement. I include a variety of case scenarios and illustrations to convey the nature of these beliefs and the methods teachers can use to promote and nurture them.

Reader Reflection – 2.1 Sparking Students' Desire to Learn

Student motivation, which can be thought of as a person's desire to engage, display effort, and persist during an activity, is a topic of great interest to teachers. In thinking about your students, answer the following questions:

- Do any of your students display poor motivation?

- What do you think are the primary causes of their poor motivation?

- Is there anything that you do to motivate your students? Be specific!

- How effective are you in motivating them to learn?

Introduction to Motivation

Over the past decade, I have been invited to provide numerous professional development workshops to educators and school personnel regarding SRL and motivation issues. Because student motivational issues and regulatory skill deficits are recognized as core problems in today's schools (Cleary, 2009; Coalition for Psychology, 2006), the volume of these requests has not been particularly surprising. What did surprise, however, was the wide range of schools and organizations that have been interested in these issues. For example, over the past decade, I have conducted SRL-related workshops in preschools and elementary schools, middle and high schools, community colleges, four-year colleges, and even medical schools. I have come to realize that regardless of the specific context, most educators are thirsting for guidance in how to influence their students' intrinsic desire and motivation to improve in school.

I have thoroughly enjoyed providing these workshops because teachers are a fun group to work with and because I recognize the potential influence and importance of the teacher–student relationship. Teachers serve on the front lines with students and serve as a key agent for change; not just in terms of the content that students learn, but the ways in which students think about themselves and their capabilities in school. The importance of the student–teacher dynamic has been well documented in the research literature (Eccles & Roeser, 2011; Wentzel, 2016) and has been poignantly displayed in cinema, such as *Dead Poets Society* (1989), *Stand and Deliver* (1988), *Dangerous Minds* (1995), or *Lean on Me* (1989). In *Stand and Deliver*, the main character, Jaime Escalante (played by Edward James Olmos), is a math teacher at James A. Garfield High School in East Los Angeles who works with a class of marginalized and academically at-risk students. Although bright, many of these students exhibit poor motivation – they openly express a strong level of disinterest in school, are resistant to completing schoolwork, and do not recognize the relevance of school to their lives. Through his passion for teaching and the use of motivation-enhancing methods to alter students' maladaptive beliefs and self-perceptions, Escalante ultimately found a way to spark his students' untapped potential.

In the *Dead Poets Society*, a movie set in a very different context (a prestigious prep school in Vermont), English teacher John Keating (played by Robin Williams) uses a variety of non-traditional teaching methods to nurture his students' beliefs and perceptions about living life on their own terms. By helping his students develop their own voices and a personal sense of agency and autonomy, Keating helped his students realize that change and growth are not only possible, but are truly under their control. These movies are just two of the many films that underscore two central themes of this chapter:

- student beliefs and perceptions are important determinants of their motivation
- teachers can serve as a key agent of change for these beliefs and perceptions.

Motivation Defined

Motivation can be defined as a process through which people initiate and sustain behavior in pursuit of a goal (Schunk, Meece, & Pintrich, 2014). It typically is

Motivation: Fueling the SRL Loop

Table 2.1 Overview of key sources of motivated behaviors

Motivation belief	Definition	Link to motivated behaviors
Self-efficacy	beliefs about one's ability to perform specific behaviors	"I try hard when something is difficult because I **believe that I can** eventually get it"
Instrumentality/value	beliefs regarding the importance or value of a task or behavior	"I study a lot because **it is important** that I get good grades and go to college"
Interest	the level of perceived enjoyment or interest in a given activity	"I participate in class discussions because they are **enjoyable**"
Growth mindset	beliefs that ability or intelligence can change with effort and practice	"I persist on these assignments because I know **my skills can improve with practice**"
Autonomy	perceptions that one can make choices about one's behaviors and learning	"I am motivated to do my homework because **I have some say or choice** in how to do it"

represented by the things that propel us to act as well as the nature of these actions; whether such actions are observable (e.g., going to extra help sessions after school, studying for three hours the night before an exam) or covert (e.g., using self-talk to motivate oneself to learn when bored).

The guiding principle in this chapter is that teachers can directly influence student motivation (i.e., effort, persistence, choice) by helping them learn more adaptive ways of thinking about themselves and the process of learning. I highlight five widely recognized sources of motivation: self-efficacy, interest, value or instrumentality, growth mindset, and perceptions of autonomy (see Table 2.1).

General Thoughts About Motivation in Schools

Before delving into each of these motivational sources and the specific approaches that can enhance them, there are a few important caveats to keep in mind. First, although I place primary attention on motivation in this chapter, I also address it (at least on some level) in most chapters. For example, I highlight the motivational influence of students' causal attributions (Chapter 7) and goal-setting (Chapter 4) and then discuss how teacher feedback (Chapter 5) and student self-monitoring (Chapter 6) can influence students' desire to learn. Finally, in multiple chapters throughout this book, I illustrate how student–teacher relations also play a role in student motivation.

It is also important to note that motivation is a *malleable* construct – that is, it can change over time via natural experiences or from instructional activities and interventions (Pajares & Urdan, 2006; Schunk et al., 2014; Schunk & Zimmerman, 2008). Due to its malleable nature, I personally reject the mindset or perspective that sometimes creeps into the heads of educators, such as "some students just don't have it" or "they are simply unmotivated and lazy kids." From my viewpoint, all children can become more cognitively engaged, motivated learners – the trick is figuring out how to do this in real time with kids who do not want to engage and who resist completing their work.

A third point is that the five motivational beliefs discussed in this chapter have been shown by researchers to positively influence students' behaviors and/or achievement; thus, it is fair to say that each of them represents some part or piece of the motivation puzzle (Schunk & Zimmerman, 2008). Further, these processes are closely intertwined, and tend to reciprocally influence each other (e.g., autonomy-support influences student interest and vice versa). Thus, as you read this chapter, I encourage you to consider how you can *concurrently* target multiple motivation beliefs rather than one or two beliefs in isolation (Linnenbrink-Garcia & Patall, 2016). In the movie *Stand and Deliver*, Escalante did this very thing. Over time, he got his students to recognize the value of academic success to their lives (*perceived value*) and to believe that their intelligence was not fixed (*growth mindset*). He also helped his students become more aware of the actual successes that they were having in school, which helped them to become more confident in their ability to succeed (*self-efficacy*). By influencing these different beliefs, Escalante was able to get many of his students to recognize and display the effort and hard work needed to perform at a higher level.

Finally, the five motivation beliefs addressed in this chapter do not represent an exhaustive list of all potential motivational determinants. Due to space limitations, I was not able to address other important motivational processes (e.g., goal orientation, future selves), nor was I able to sufficiently address the effects of sociocultural norms (i.e., the culture students are from) and other socio-contextual factors (e.g., effects of poverty; King & McInerney, 2016) on student motivation.

Core Concept 2.1

The first key step in becoming an effective "motivator" is to develop a strong working knowledge of the array of motivation beliefs and/or perceptions that influence student behavior.

Self-Efficacy – How Well Can I Do These Things?

Self-efficacy, which is similar to the more colloquial term self-confidence, represents a person's beliefs in his or her ability to display specific behaviors at a certain level of performance during a given situation or task (Bandura, 1997). Self-efficacy does not pertain to a person's overall confidence ("I am a good student and will do well in school"). Rather, it is very specific and can vary across different assignments or activities. For example, it is possible for Tanya to believe that she can successfully solve a specific set of mathematics problems but to also display self-doubts about her ability to learn and recall information for social studies exams.

Self-efficacy beliefs should also not be confused with self-esteem. The latter term pertains to people's feelings about themselves in terms of their worth or personal qualities valued in society (e.g., "I am a kind person," "I am attractive and likeable"; Bandura, 1997). Obviously, we all want our students to feel positively about themselves and to believe that they are worthy of recognition and attention (self-esteem). However, I have elected to focus specifically on self-efficacy because it is one of the strongest predictors of adaptive academic behaviors and outcomes (Bandura, 1997; Pajares & Urdan, 2006).

How Can You Influence Student Self-Efficacy?

Bandura (1986) discussed four primary sources of self-efficacy: *mastery experiences* (successfully performing a behavior), *vicarious experiences* (watching similar others perform a behavior), *verbal persuasion* (being told that you can do it), and *physiological experiences* (observing biological or physiological reactions to situations). Of these determinants, mastery experiences are typically viewed as the most powerful. In other words, students are most likely to believe that they can accomplish something or get things done when they experience repeated "demonstrations of success." This principle of demonstrated success extends well beyond the academic realm, such as sports and other fields. In his book, *Finding a Way To Win*, Hall of Fame football coach Bill Parcells commented on motivation stating, "People don't get it from fancy pep talks, or psychological string-pulling, or positive thinking handbooks ... Confidence is only born of demonstrated ability" (Parcells, 1995, p. 86). Although this statement minimizes the potential short-term motivational impact of supportive comments and encouragement from others, I fully endorse the point that when people experience frequent success, their confidence will likely strengthen. In this section, I address how teachers can increase the number of opportunities for students to experience repeated success.

Demonstrated Success – Tip #1: Create multiple opportunities for students to "see" progress

An effective way to help students experience success is to provide them with multiple opportunities to do so. Every performance situation represents a potential opportunity for students to ask themselves, Am I competent at doing this activity? In my experience, there is great variability in the number, types, and complexity of learning activities that teachers assign students. Some teachers may administer weekly quizzes as well as unit exams to their students whereas others may only assign unit exams or other long-term assignments, such as writing a research paper. The latter situation is particularly problematic for struggling students. As the number of performance opportunities *decrease*, the weight or influence of these outcomes on students' overall grades *increase* – that is, each outcome is weighted much more heavily. Of greater concern is that when performance situations are infrequent, students will have less of an opportunity to demonstrate growth or improvement in their skills.

> **Core Concept 2.2**
>
> To maximize student confidence, increase the number of opportunities they have to display instances of success and mastery.

Demonstrated Success – Tip #2: Break down complex tasks into component parts or skills

As I discuss extensively in Chapter 7, when students receive feedback about course assignments, such as a long-term research paper or a unit exam in mathematics, they tend to focus all of their attention on the specific grade. Most students will not sift through the assignment to identify patterns of mistakes that they made or to pinpoint specific areas in which they excelled. They will need some prompting or a nudge to do so. From my perspective, teachers can bolster students' self-efficacy by providing them with more detailed or nuanced information about performance via a scoring rubric or subscores for different parts of an assignment. By breaking down a learning activity into component parts and then providing performance information about each component, teachers will increase the odds that most students will notice at least some instances of demonstrated success (see Tales of the Student – 2.1).

Tales of the Student – 2.1 Peter

Approximately every four to five weeks, Peter's science teacher, Ms. Johnson, asks her students to complete a science investigation (lab exercise). Ms. Johnson gives students an overall grade for each lab report (0–100 points) but also writes the number of points that students earned on each section. Unfortunately, Peter has been struggling on these activities; he earned grades of 79, 70, and 75 on the previous three labs. Peter was quite frustrated because of his inability to improve his grades. Although Ms. Johnson provided students with a breakdown of the overall grade across lab sections (procedures, analysis, results, etc.), Peter did not pay attention to this more nuanced scoring. He was simply too upset with the overall grade. To help re-direct Peter's focus and attention to the scoring breakdown, Mr. Gebbia (Peter's guidance counselor) asked Peter to use a monitoring form to record the number of points earned across the lab sections for the prior three labs (see Table 2.2). Mr. Gebbia asked Peter to complete the table and to come see him at the end of the school day. The following exchange ensued:

Mr. Gebbia: *So what did you think about this form I had you complete?*

Peter: *I don't really know. My grade was bad but it looked like I did some things well.*

Mr. Gebbia: *What do you mean about doing some things well?*

Peter: *On the experimental procedures and format I did not lose as many points.*

Mr. Gebbia: *So what does that mean to you?*

Peter: *Well, the overall grade is still pretty bad, so who really cares how I did on these two parts?*

Mr. Gebbia: *I understand what you mean and I do agree that your overall grade is not what you want. But it is important that you see that you performed at an A-level on the experimental procedures and format sections. On some of the labs, you have also done well on the results section. So, on 3 of the 5 sections you have shown mastery or very good skills.*

Peter: *Huh … I guess I see your point. But I still did bad on the assignment.*

Mr. Gebbia: *I do realize that … but the overall grade does not tell the entire story. You are doing well in some areas, but the key question now becomes, what do you need to focus on to improve the analysis and conclusion sections? If we can figure that out, your grades will likely be much higher.*

Even though Peter's overall grade was not what he wanted, because he was able to evaluate his performance across each part of the lab, he recognized that his overall grades of 79, 70, and 75 did not accurately reflect his skills and knowledge. His exchange with Mr. Gebbia led him to feel more efficacious and enhanced his awareness of skills that he needed to improve. Just to be clear, however, I am not advocating that teachers or other school staff should distort reality for students or have them ignore the

Table 2.2 Peter's performance on science labs over time

Section of Lab (total points)	Lab #1 Points earned	Lab #2 Points earned	Lab #3 Points earned	Points earned/ Total possible points
Experimental procedures (25)	23/25	22/25	23/25	68/75 = 90.7%
Analysis (25)	15/25	13/25	12/25	40/75 = 53.3%
Results (25)	22/25	15/25	19/25	56/75 = 74.6%
Conclusion (15)	10/15	10/15	12/15	32/45 = 71.1%
Format (10 points)	9/10	10/10	9/10	28/30 = 93.3%
TOTAL points	79/100	70/100	75/100	

importance or relevance of a poor grade on an assignment. I am simply underscoring the value of helping students develop a more nuanced understanding of the grades they receive on assignments.

Core Concept 2.3

Even when students struggle on a task, you can build their self-efficacy by helping them notice or "see" the specific things they have mastered or performed well.

Demonstrated Success – Tip #3: Informal and personal messages of mastery

Developing student self-efficacy is not confined to situations when they receive a grade on an assignment or test. Teachers can enhance student efficacy informally by pointing out instances of mastery and competence during classroom-based learning activities. In many of the courses that I teach, I occasionally write emails to students to convey my observations about the competency or quality of their behaviors or skills. In fact, during one semester, I had a student who frequently participated in class discussions and provided incredibly useful and insightful comments about the topic of discussion. To make her aware of these specific adaptive behaviors and to convey efficacy-related information about them, I wrote her a short email identifying the specific behaviors that were exemplary (i.e., providing insightful comments) and explained why and how this behavior demonstrated competency or skill. Taking a minute or two to provide students with these types of efficacy-enhancing messages can have powerful effects on their "can do" perceptions.

Task Values – Is This Enjoyable and Important to Me?

Expectancy-value researchers have contributed tremendously to our understanding of human motivation (Eccles & Wigfield, 2002; Fredericks & Eccles, 2002). From this perspective, people tend to take on challenging tasks when they expect to perform well in the future (expectancies) and when the activity is perceived to be valuable or important (task values). Given that expectancies and self-efficacy overlap to some degree, I focus my attention here on task values; that is, the extent to which students perceive tasks as being enjoyable or valuable.

Broadly speaking, students will value engaging in a learning activity when they find it enjoyable or interesting (*task interest*), perceive the activity to be important and relevant to their lives (*instrumentality*), view the activity to be an integral part of who they are (*attainment*), and/or believe that the activity is not overly burdensome (*cost*; Eccles & Wigfield, 2002). Although each dimension is important, I focus on the interest and instrumentality dimensions.

There is compelling literature demonstrating the positive influence of student perceptions of interest and value (Hidi & Ainley, 2008; Schunk et al., 2014). In general, students who show greater enjoyment and interest in an activity exhibit positive emotions, high levels of attention, and adaptive approaches to learning, including high levels of persistence when challenged. Along a similar vein, students who believe that a learning activity will lead to desirable consequences (e.g., studying hard will lead to better grades which can lead to getting into a good college) will often persist when challenged, exhibit deeper levels of processing, and will likely make choices to become deeply engaged in that activity (Eccles & Wigfield, 2002; Hidi & Ainley, 2008; Schunk et al., 2014).

●●●●●

How Can You Develop and Enhance Student Interest?

We all want to do things that we find interesting, exciting, or enjoyable. While it is not realistic for students to enjoy everything about school, it is possible for teachers to stimulate their interest. As you read this section, it is important that you ask yourself two fundamental questions: "How can I spark an *initial* level of interest in my students?" and "How can I help students *sustain* that level of interest over time?" Thus, developing interest among students does not simply involve doing "fun" things or capturing student interest at the outset of a learning activity. It also involves strategically and purposefully doing things to help students maintain that interest over time (Hidi & Ainley, 2008).

Sparking initial interest. One effective tactic is to make the learning context or activities appealing to students on both a cognitive (thinking) and affective (emotion) level. That is, devise classroom environments or learning activities that get students to attend to the task and to experience positive emotions. As a general rule of thumb, do things that instill a sense of fun, creativity, and excitement for students (see Tales of the Teacher – 2.1).

Tales of the Teacher – 2.1 Ms. Johnson

Ms. Johnson is a 9th grade life sciences teacher who includes natural selection as a topic in her courses. As part of the broader curriculum on this topic, Ms. Johnson requires her students to complete a lab activity supplemented by videos, small group activities, and other tasks. In one of the video clips, the Galapagos species are presented to illustrate key ideas related to natural selection. To get students excited about watching this short video clip she embedded a theme song from a video game that her students really like. The song also relates to the overarching message related to the overall purpose of the lesson. By combining the use of interesting videos plus the added component of an enjoyable song that is familiar to students, Ms. Johnson has had much success in eliciting an initial burst of excitement and positive emotion from the students – the key *first* step (but not the only step) in the interest-enhancement process.

Sustaining interest over time. After the initial experiences of interest and excitement begin to wane for students (and this will almost always happen), it is important that you now begin to focus on *maintaining* student interest over time. Hidi and Reninger (2006) noted that to develop sustained interest it is important to get students to connect with the content or specific learning activity in a more personal and meaningful way (see Tales of the Teacher – 2.2).

Tales of the Teacher – 2.2 Ms. Johnson

As part of a science investigation, Ms. Johnson uses a variety of hands-on activities related to natural selection, such as having students place different-colored beans in bags or reading interesting passages about the process of natural selection. She will also ask students to make several predictions about the results of the experiments so that they can be more active in evaluating themselves during the lab. Collectively, these aspects of the learning situation are designed to get students to become more cognitively engaged and interested in course content. With enhanced personal interest, it is likely that students will reflect more deeply on the content and may even question why their initial conceptions or predictions were off (see Table 2.3 for more detailed information about strategies for improving interest).

How Can You Help Students Perceive Tasks as Valuable?

Students can enjoy a given learning activity and find it both stimulating and interesting; however, their motivation to persist and engage may decline if they do not believe the activity is relevant or meaningful in some way. It is important to get students to see that performing well on the learning activity will lead to something desirable: better grades, enhanced knowledge on a topic of interest, more effective life skills, etc. Personally, I attempt to apply this principle when teaching my courses. I have come to learn that my doctoral students possess a wide range of long-term career interests and aspirations. Some students want to work exclusively as a school psychologist in K-12 school contexts or as a counselor in a college setting. Others wish to open up a private practice as a mental health professional, therapist, evaluator, or perhaps as an educational consultant. Because of these diverse long-term interests and goals, it is distinctly possible that some students are excited to read about learning theories and academic interventions but others are not. As a result, I spend some time at the beginning of all of my courses attempting to create a "climate of relevance." That is, I engage students in conversations about how the key concepts/topics of my courses relate to their potential career ambitions and goals. Although our students are often highly motivated and engaged, when they can clearly see the link between course content and their careers, they tend to more fully value and appreciate the topics that I cover.

There are many other ways in which teachers can enhance student perceptions of value or instrumentality about school activities (see Table 2.3). A first step is to identify things that are important to your students. What do they love to do or what is most important to them in school, both in the short term and long term? If you learn that your students value playing sports, reading about World War II planes, writing essays, going to college, or participating in chorus or band, you can more easily match course content or activities to those valued activities. In most

Table 2.3 Tactics to promote interest and value of learning activities

Ways to promote situational interest	Ways to promote perceptions of value
• Devise learning activities that lead to positive emotions • Link student interests to class topics and activities • Emphasize novelty and diversity in the tasks • Enhance student autonomy by giving choices • Emphasize real-life applications and hands-on activities • Utilize peer-based learning formats	• Provide rationales for activities • Openly discuss why learning activities are meaningful • Emphasize the link between learning activities and both short-term and long-term outcomes/consequences • Model your own interests and value for topics presented in class • Discuss levels of importance across the class, content, and type of learning activity

instances, enhancing student perceptions of value about schoolwork involves informal exchanges between a teacher and student. Consider Ms. Maino, who is Peter's 9th grade mathematics teacher. Peter has been struggling much of the semester and does not consistently complete his homework and classwork. In speaking with Peter one day, Ms. Maino discovered that Peter loves airplanes and that he wants to become an Air Force pilot or an aerospace engineer. After doing a bit of research on these potential careers, she locates a few interesting, developmentally appropriate articles and brochures that link these careers to mathematics. Following class one day, Ms. Maino hands the information to Peter and tells him to let her know if he wants to talk about how the things they do in math class relate to his interest in planes and aviation.

Core Concept 2.4

To get students interested in a learning activity, teachers should try to:

- elicit positive emotions or reactions in them when beginning the activity
- make the activity as relevant and meaningful to their lives as possible.

Reflect and Connect – 2.1 Revisiting Reader Reflection

- Based on what you have read so far in the chapter, has your understanding of motivation changed? How so?

  _____

  _____

- What challenges do you foresee having in getting your students motivated and engaged in learning?

  _____

  _____

Motivation: Fueling the SRL Loop 29

Student Autonomy: How Much of a Say Do I Have in My Learning?

Edward Deci and Richard Ryan developed a highly influential and comprehensive model of motivation and self-regulation. At the heart of their self-determination theoretical framework is the premise that student motivation will be optimized when their needs for *autonomy, competence, and relatedness* are supported and nurtured (Ryan & Deci, 2002). Of interest in this section is the extent to which students perceive themselves as autonomous individuals.

At an individual level, Webster defines autonomy as the power or right to self-govern. That is, people want the freedom to make choices; they want to do things based on their own personal interests (what they enjoy) and values (what is important to them) and will typically experience satisfaction when they can direct their own lives and assume responsibility for their behaviors. This line of thinking makes sense, but is it realistic to allow kids freedom in school or to relinquish some control in your classroom to your students? After all, as a teacher, you have a lot of content to cover and probably have come to value the need for structure, organization, clear expectations, and rules in your classroom. You may even be wondering, "Wouldn't relinquishing control to the students be a recipe for chaos?", or perhaps, "I need to have control over my classroom or else students won't learn."

Although these concerns are justified, nurturing and supporting student autonomy *does not* mean that you relinquish control of your classroom. Nor does it imply that you should always allow students to choose the topics they want to learn or to behave in any way they want without consequence. It is best to think about autonomy supports as "structured" choices and freedoms. That is, choices within the defined parameters, structure, and rules of your classroom. Before reading the remainder of this section, please complete Reflect and Connect exercise 2.2.

Reflect and Connect – 2.2 Autonomy-Supporting Practices

Supporting student autonomy can be an effective way of enhancing student motivation. To what extent have you helped your students:

- perceive that they have some control over the activities you assign?

  _____

- experience a sense of freedom rather than coercion?

  _____

  _____

- believe that they can make choices about how to complete learning activities?

  _____

  _____

How Can You Support Student Autonomy?

Before discussing empirically supported instructional tactics for promoting student auton-omy, I encourage you to consider a couple of points. First, as I emphasize in most chapters in this book, successful application of SRL and motivation principles to classroom contexts requires you to think about these principles in relation to the projects, assignments, and/ or exams you use. Thus, developing a clear and vivid sense of the things you ask students to do is a key first step in figuring out how to infuse autonomy-supportive practices relative to those activities.

Another point is that autonomy-supportive practices (as well as recommendations for all other motivation beliefs mentioned in this chapter) are not resource- or time-in-tensive. In Table 2.4, I present a list of autonomy-supportive instructional approaches (Reeve et al., 2008). In reviewing these practices, you will notice that the majority of them pertain to social-emotional behaviors and skills that we hope all teachers would naturally exhibit, such as being empathic, engaging in active listening, and being responsive to student needs.

Another interesting aspect of autonomy-supports is that they typically entail mak-ing *minor* changes to classroom discourse or types of assignments or activities. In Table 2.5, I present four brief case scenarios to illustrate the relative simplicity with which you can infuse these practices in your classroom. As a general rule of thumb, when attempting to promote student autonomy, you should first distinguish between the essential (non-negotiable with students) and non-essential (negotiated with stu-dents) aspects of the activities. Then give students choices and freedom about these non-essential or negotiable components.

Table 2.4 Empirically validated autonomy-supportive practices

Autonomy-supportive instructional practices	
Listening	Time teacher spends listening to students' voice during instruction
Asking what students want, need	Frequency with which teacher asks what the students want or need
Creating independent work time	Time teacher allows students to work independently and in their own way
Encouraging students' voice	Time students spend talking about the lesson during instruction
Seating arrangement	The provision of seating arrangements in which the students – rather than the teacher – are positioned near the learning materials
Providing rationales	Frequency with which teacher provides rationales to explain why a particular course of action, way of thinking, or way of feeling might be useful
Praise as informational feedback	Frequency of statements to communicate positive effective feedback about students' improvement or mastery
Offering encouragement	Frequency of statements to boost or sustain students' engagement (e.g., "You can do it")
Offering hints	Frequency of suggestions about how to make progress when students seem stuck
Being responsive	Being responsive to student-generated questions, comments, recommendations, and suggestions
Perspective-taking statements	Frequency of empathic statements to acknowledge the students' perspective or experiences

Source: From "Understanding and promoting autonomous self-regulation: A self-determination theory per-spective." In D. H. Schunk & B. J. Zimmerman (Eds.) (2008), *Motivation and self-regulated learning: Theory, research, and applications* (p. 231). New York: Lawrence Erlbaum Associates. Adapted with permission.

Motivation: Fueling the SRL Loop

Table 2.5 Illustrations of autonomy-supporting practices across classroom contexts

Examples of autonomy-supportive instructional practices	How the practice cultivates autonomy
Mr. Miller is a 6th grade English teacher who has three things he wants to accomplish during class on Monday. After telling students about the day's objectives, he asks them to identify the activity that they want to do first. He also told them that they could work on one activity for 15 minutes, and the other two activities for only 8–10 minutes.	Students are given *choices* about two dimensions of a specific task (the order and length of time to complete each activity).
Mr. Spinner is a 9th grade science teacher. As part of a two-day lesson on the circulatory system, he lets his class decide about one of the activities on Day 1. Students can either watch a video of the circulatory system that is kid friendly and plays current pop music, or they can help to make the classroom into the circulatory system using balloons as props for oxygen or carbon dioxide. For Day 2, he allows each student to spend 15 minutes of independent time to reflect on what they learned the previous day. The students can either write their response, draw a picture to convey their ideas, or can have a small group conversation with the teacher to discuss the activity.	The session taps into students' *personal interests* (authentic, interesting activities) and provides them *freedom* and *flexibility* (independent reflection activity) when engaging in an activity. It also allows for student *choice* about the learning activity on Day 1 and the method for expressing their learning on Day 2.
Ms. Cetta is an 11th grade calculus teacher. She is an excellent teacher, but recently learned that many of her former students felt that she was excessively controlling and critical of their behaviors. Realizing that her behaviors might be undermining student motivation, she develops a strategy to guide autonomy-supportive practices when interacting with her students (LIVE): L (Listen), I (Invite questions), V (students Voice), and E (show Empathy).	Combines four specific autonomy-supportive behaviors that collectively validate and support students' realities and experiences – *listening*, *encouraging student voice*, *inviting questions*, and *empathy*.
Ms. Garcia is a 4th grade teacher. At the beginning of the school year, Ms. Garcia collaborated with her students about a plan or routine for beginning each school day. It was decided that upon entering the classroom, students can have 15 minutes to work on any of three activities: read a book, finish classwork from previous day, or go on the computer to practice fluency skills. She also told the class that they can change the activities at various points throughout the school year, if desired.	Students' *internal locus of control* is emphasized in that the students helped to design the plan and can make suggestions about changing the three activities throughout the year. Students are also given *choice* about which of the three activities they could select.

> **Core Concept 2.5**
>
> When trying to support student autonomy, identify what you perceive to be the *negotiable* (non-essential) and *non-negotiable* (essential) aspects of an assignment; then provide students with choices and freedom about the *negotiable* things.

● ● ● ● ●

Growth Mindset: Can My Capacity Grow and Improve?

One of the most debilitating experiences for students is that moment of realization that they lack the ability to improve or to control their lives in some way. That is, some students develop a mindset that their abilities are fixed, and that no matter what they do they will not be able to change how smart or good they are at something. For the past several decades, Carol Dweck has conducted research to explore how students react to challenge and failure. She has also examined why some students, regardless of ability, respond positively to challenge yet others fall victim to more negative and maladaptive ways of thinking. Central to her theory of motivation is that the way people conceptualize or view the nature of intelligence (or one's overall ability) will directly influence their approach and motivation to learn (Dweck, 2000).

In general, students who believe that intelligence is fixed (*fixed mindset*) tend to play it safe. They will often become overly concerned with failure or looking bad in front of others. From this perspective, mistakes represent signs of poor ability that need to be avoided at all costs. Conversely, students who exhibit a more incremental or malleable view of intelligence (*growth mindset*) tend to embrace challenge and difficulty. These types of students are motivated to learn simply for the sake of learning and are likely to view mistakes as a natural part of the learning process. Students with a growth mindset also will likely judge success in terms of personal progress or improvement rather than outperforming others. This latter distinction is important because when students focus on norms (outperforming others) they are more likely to experience negative emotion and stress in school (see Chapter 7).

● ● ● ● ●

How Can You Cultivate a Growth Mindset in Students?

Several decades of research have shown that student perceptions of intelligence or ability can be altered with simple yet powerful messages about the link between the brain, learning, and effort (Dweck, 2000; Blackwell, Trzesniewski, & Dweck, 2007). Dweck and colleagues have developed an intervention approach that focuses on teaching students that the brain is malleable and that practice and effort can cause changes in the brain that make people "smarter". As part of this intervention, students are provided a series of motivating and empowering messages that collectively underscore the importance of adopting a growth mindset (see Table 2.6 for example messages).

Unlike students exhibiting a fixed mindset, those with a growth mindset focus on displaying improvement or progress. They also tend to believe that challenging tasks are interesting and fun. A growth mindset intervention will typically create opportunities for students to observe growth in their knowledge or skills so that they come to believe that change is possible. As I will highlight in Chapter 7, a growth mindset approach is similar to that of attribution retraining interventions. In these latter interventions, students are taught to think about their success and failures in terms of malleable or controllable factors, like effort and strategy use, rather than innate ability or other fixed factors. The basic idea is that student motivation will be enhanced when they believe that performance outcomes are under their control rather than pre-determined by innate factors.

I present two case scenarios to further convey the meaning of growth and fixed mindsets (see Tales of the Teacher – 2.3 and 2.4). Before reading the two scenarios, however, take a look at Reflect and Connect exercise 2.3.

Table 2.6 Examples of growth-mindset messages

Growth-mindset messages

"Thinking and learning can change the brain"

"The brain is a muscle that gets stronger with practice"

"Making mistakes is an important part of learning"

"Being smart is a choice that we make"

Motivation: Fueling the SRL Loop

Reflect and Connect – 2.3 Promoting a Growth Mindset

As you read the scenarios about Ms. Plank and Mr. Presto, I would like you to reflect on the specific instructional tactics they used to cultivate a growth mindset in students.

- What do you think about these tactics or approaches? Are they realistic and feasible to use in your classroom?

Tales of the Teacher – 2.3 Ms. Plank

Ms. Plank is a 5th grade elementary school teacher. At a recent meeting with all 4th and 5th grade teachers at her school, Ms. Plank expressed concern to her colleagues about the large number of students who exhibit a "helpless" pattern of thinking and behavior in her class. That is, after a poor grade on a writing assignment or a vocabulary quiz, her students are quick to label themselves as "dumb" or "stupid." What was surprising is that many students do these things even after performing well on previous assignments. It is as if many of her students are preoccupied with how intelligent or smart they are and view each poor grade as reflecting their weak skills and abilities. Mr. Boord, one of Ms. Plank's colleagues, suggested that she try using graphing procedures to help students obtain a more realistic understanding of their performance. From his experience, students with that helpless pattern often display a distorted sense of how they perform in school – that is, they often overestimate their failures and underestimate their successes. In his class, Mr. Boord frequently asks students to make graphs that depict their grades on different types of assignments (quizzes, writing assignments). Because most of his students display different patterns of success and struggle across these assignments, the graph becomes a great conversation tool about student perceptions of their growth (see Chapter 6 for example graphs).

Tales of the Teacher – 2.4 Mr. Presto

Mr. Presto teaches pre-calculus and calculus classes at a local high school. In teaching these courses over the past several years, he has noticed that a fairly large number of students become "fearful" when asked to solve challenging problems. Many of these students get embarrassed if they make mistakes and tend to view mistakes as a sign that they are not very good at mathematics. Of particular concern to Mr. Presto is that many of these students are at-risk for dropping his class or for not enrolling in more advanced courses as they progress through school. To help "normalize" making mistakes for his students and to reinforce the idea that their ability to perform complex math is not a fixed entity, Mr. Presto decides to tell his students a series of "success" stories. He often talked about former students who had initially struggled in his class, but through perseverance and effort, became "smarter" in doing calculus. He would tell these stories at the beginning of each semester, but would also deliver these messages when students needed a "pep talk" or reminder about adaptive ways of thinking. To make his message even more powerful, Mr. Presto also had former students, who had initially struggled but eventually improved, visit his classes to share their stories.

Figure 2.1 Instructional prompt for motivation processes

• • • • •

Concluding Thoughts

I covered a lot of ground in this chapter. However, I wanted to make sure that you remember to keep in mind three key ideas when attempting to motivate your students.

Ask yourself the right motivational questions. As you all know, a day in the life of a teacher is busy and oftentimes chaotic. Thus, you may not be able to devote a lot of time to reflecting on why your students may or may not be motivated. To make this process a bit more efficient and straightforward, use Figure 2.1 to remind yourself about important motivation-related questions that can guide your thinking. Just make sure that you reflect on these questions in relation to the learning activities that you emphasize in your classroom.

Core Concept 2.6

All teachers possess the capacity and skill to provide *motivation-enhancing messages* to their students. Do the best you can in learning about different motivation beliefs and then think about how you can target several of these beliefs when working with students.

Remind yourself that motivation is a multi-faceted construct. To be able to enhance student motivation (i.e., effort, persistence, etc.), you need to help students see that change or growth is possible and under their control (i.e., self-efficacy, growth mindset, autonomy) and that learning can be an exciting and valuable activity (i.e., interest, perceived instrumentality). Does this mean that you need to consider all of these processes when working with students across all learning activities or under all circumstances? Of course not; no teacher will be able to focus on all of these processes for all students. However, the general idea is that you will probably have greater success in motivating your students when you are knowledgeable about the different sources of motivation, and are able to concurrently target several of them (Linnenbrink-Garcia & Patall, 2016). Thus, be sure to continually develop and expand on your "motivational toolkit."

Become a good listener, observer, and evaluator. In addition to developing a solid understanding of the various motivation beliefs, teachers need to increase their awareness about the beliefs that are most problematic for particular students. Students will routinely make comments and/or display non-verbal behaviors that convey messages about their underlying motivation beliefs and processes. Pay attention to these verbalizations and actions because they can give insight into the particular motivation processes that you may want or need to target.

⬤ ⬤ ⬤ ⬤ ⬤

REFERENCES

Bandura, A. (1986). *Social foundations of thought and action: A social cognitive theory.* Englewood Cliffs, NJ: Prentice Hall.

Bandura, A. (1997). *Self-efficacy: The exercise of control.* New York, NY: W. H. Freeman.

Blackwell, L. S., Trzesniewski, K. H., & Dweck, C. S. (2007). Implicit theories of intelligence predict achievement across an adolescent transition: A longitudinal and an intervention. *Child Development, 78*(1), 246–263.

Cleary, T. J. (2009). School-based motivation and self-regulation assessments: An examination of school psychologist beliefs and practices. *Journal of Applied School Psychology, 25*(1), 71–94. doi:10.1080/15377900802484190.

Coalition for Psychology in Schools and Education. (2006, August). *Report on the teacher needs survey.* Washington, DC: American Psychological Association, Center for Psychology in Schools and Education.

Dweck, C. S. (2000). *Self-Theories: Their role in motivation, personality, and development. Essays in Social Psychology.* New York: Psychology Press.

Eccles, J. S., & Wigfield, A. (2002). Motivational beliefs, values, and goals. *Annual Review of Psychology, 53*(1), 109.

Eccles, J. S., & Roeser, R. W. (2011). Schools as developmental contexts during adolescence. *Journal of Research on Adolescence, 21*(1), 225–241. doi:10.1111/j.1532–7795.2010.00725.x.

Fredericks, J., & Eccles, J. S. (2002). Children's competence and value beliefs from children through adolescence: Growth trajectories in two male sex-typed domains. *Developmental Psychology, 38,* 519–533.

Hidi, S., & Ainley, M. (2008). Interest and self-regulation: Relationship between two variables that influence learning. In D. H. Schunk and B. J. Zimmerman (Eds.), *Motivation and self-regulated learning: Theory, research, and applications* (pp. 77–109). New York: Lawrence Erlbaum Associates.

Hidi, S., & Reninger, K. A. (2006). The four-phase model of interest development. *Educational Psychologist, 41,* 111–127.

King, R. B., & McInerney, D. M. (2016). Culture and motivation: The road traveled and the way ahead. In K. R. Wentzel & D. B. Miele (Eds.), *Handbook of motivation at school* (pp. 275–299). New York: Routledge.

Linnenbrink-Garcia, L., & Patall, E. A. (2016). Motivation. In L. Corno & E. M. Anderman (Eds.), *Handbook of educational psychology* (3rd ed.) (pp. 91–103). New York: Routledge.

Pajares, F., & Urdan, T. (2006). *Self-efficacy beliefs of adolescents.* Greenwich, CT: Information Age Publishing.

Parcells, B. (1995). *Finding a way to win: The principles of leadership, teamwork, and motivation.* New York: Doubleday.

Reeve, J., Ryan, R., Deci, E. L., & Jang, H. (2008). Understanding and promoting autonomous self-regulation: A self-determination theory perspective. In D. H. Schunk and B. J. Zimmerman (Eds.), *Motivation and self-regulated learning: Theory, research, and applications* (pp. 223–244). New York: Lawrence Erlbaum Associates.

Ryan, R. M., & Deci, E. L. (2002). An overview of self-determination theory: An organismic-dialectical perspective. In E. L. Deci & R. M. Ryan (Eds.), *Handbook of Self-determination research* (pp. 3–33). Rochester, NY: University of Rochester Press.

Schunk, D. H., Meece, J. L., & Pintrich, P. R. (2014). *Motivation in education: Theory, research, and applications* (4th ed.). Upper Saddle River, NJ: Pearson Education.

Schunk, D. H., & Zimmerman, B. J. (2008). *Motivation and self-regulated learning: Theory, research, and applications.* New York: Lawrence Erlbaum Associates.

Wentzel, K. R. (2016). Teacher–student relationships. In K. R Wentzel and D. B Miele (Eds.), *Handbook of motivation at school* (2nd ed.) (pp. 211–230). New York: Routledge.

3

Strategies: Tools for Directing the SRL Loop

I believe that people make their own luck by great preparation and good strategy.
—Jack Canfield

 Chapter Snapshot

Thus far, I have provided a conceptual overview of SRL (Chapter 1) and underscored several motivational processes underlying the process of regulation (Chapter 2). In the final chapter of this "foundational" section, I shift my focus to another core aspect of SRL – *strategic thinking and action*. In addition to describing the meaning of a strategy, I offer several guidelines that teachers can use to help students become more purposeful and strategic as they learn. At the heart of this chapter (and the remainder of the book) is helping teachers recognize the value of getting their students to THINK IN THE LANGUAGE OF STRATEGIES.

Reader Reflection – 3.1 Strategic Thinking

In recent years, researchers and educators have focused a lot of attention on the importance of students becoming more strategic as they learn.

- How would you define a *strategy*? Do you think there are different types of strategies?

  _____

  _____

- To what extent do you explicitly teach strategies that help your students complete assignments, projects, or classroom-based learning activities?

  _____

  _____

- Do you explicitly use the phrase "strategies" when talking about the needed procedures to perform an activity?

  _____

  _____

Introduction: What Is a Strategy?

Let's first discuss the meaning of a strategy. Many labels have been used in the literature to represent strategic thinking or behaviors, such as *learning strategies, cognitive strategies, task strategies, metacognitive strategies,* and *self-regulated learning strategies.* Other phrases, such as *learning techniques, tactics,* or *procedures,* have also been emphasized. Although there are distinctions among these terms, there is also quite a bit of overlap. In a basic sense, most of these strategy-related terms reflect the things that people think and/or do in order to enhance their learning, knowledge, and/or performance on some learning activity. Pressley and Harris (2008) echoed this line of thinking, "Strategies are knowledge of procedures, knowledge about how to do something – how to decode a word, comprehend a story better, compose more completely and coherently, play first base better, and so on" (p 77). I like this description of a strategy because in addition to being fairly straightforward, it clearly underscores the connection between learning activities and the methods or procedures needed to complete them. Thus, a strategy is something that helps students think in a purposeful and specific way as they approach and complete a learning activity. I also like Pressley and Harris' (2008) description because it suggests that the strategy concept extends beyond school or academic contexts and does not relate to a certain type of activity; rather, strategies apply to virtually any activity that involves some type of process or a set of procedures.

> **Core Concept 3.1**
>
> Strategies reflect the procedures, methods, or approaches needed to perform a specific activity. It is important for teachers to identify the strategies that are directly linked to the core learning activities used in their classes.

Students as Strategic Learners

As noted in Chapter 1, SRLers strategically approach, engage, and reflect on a learning activity. The unfortunate reality, however, is that most students do not approach their schoolwork in this way, in part because they do not possess the requisite strategic knowledge and skills nor the level of persistence and effort needed to do so (see Tales of the Student – 3.1).

> **Tales of the Student – 3.1 Tanya**
>
> Tanya recently got back a mathematics test from her teacher, Ms. Martinez. She received a 72 on the test, which is consistent with her overall test average in mathematics. When discussing the test with her tutor, Tanya indicated that she did not know why she performed that way. "I was getting many of the practice problems correct in class so I don't know what happened." As the tutor looked over the exam, he noticed mistakes in how Tanya approached many of the problems. He pointed to a couple of the problems on the exam and asked, "What is the strategy that you were using when solving the problems?" Tanya looked puzzled and asked, "What do you mean? What strategy?" The tutor further probed Tanya regarding her approach to studying for the exam, "Well … how did you study for the exam? Did you do anything specific?" Tanya looked at the tutor but did not immediately respond. Finally, she simply shrugged her shoulders and said, "I just read over my notes like I always do".

Although most students will naturally exhibit some growth in their strategic knowledge and skills as they progress through school, many of them will not show substantive improvements without some type of external support (e.g., modeling, coaching, etc.); Butler, Schnellert, & Perry, 2017; Cleary, Velardi, & Schnaidman, 2017). This is problematic because when students do not understand how to strategically approach or complete a learning activity, they will often perform poorly and display negative emotional and cognitive reactions, such as frustration, self-doubts, and withdrawal. For example, although Johanna is a very bright and capable student, she will likely experience much stress and difficulty in high school and beyond if she continues to rigidly adhere to her fairly superficial approach to learning (see Tales of the Student – 3.2). A primary goal of this chapter is to enhance your knowledge of the various types of strategies that can optimize student learning in school, and the methods that you can use to entice students to use these strategies.

Tales of the Student – 3.2 Johanna

Johanna is a bright student who historically has performed very well in school. However, she has had some ups and downs in the 11th grade. She is currently enrolled in several challenging courses and is nervous because the study strategies that have worked for her in the past do not seem to be working well this year. Her typical approach to studying for exams is to memorize all key terms, to read her notes until she can recite them from memory, and to spend three to four hours studying the night before the test. Although Johanna is highly motivated, she is confused because her high level of motivation is not leading to the results that she expects and desires. Currently, whenever Johanna receives a grade on a test or project that is below her expectations, she perseverates on the grade and is flooded with self-doubts. What makes this especially difficult for Johanna is that she tends to get "stuck" in how she approaches her studies and does not always know how to adapt.

Are There Different Types of Strategies?

A strategy is an umbrella term that includes a wide range of procedures, tactics, or approaches to learning. In the literature, different strategy models or frameworks have been developed. One popular taxonomy is grounded in the premise that strategies can be differentiated based on how well they facilitate processing of information; collectively, these strategies are called *cognitive strategies*. In short, students who process information in an organized, conceptual, and personally meaningful way will have a greater chance of learning and recalling that information than students who use less sophisticated approaches (Weinstein & Mayer, 1986). Thus, students who use rote cognitive strategies, such as memorizing definitions or reading over their class notes, will often not learn information as well as those who use elaborative or sophisticated strategies, such as relating information to prior knowledge, summarizing text, or using graphic organizers.

Other taxonomies have focused on procedures and methods called *SRL strategies*. Zimmerman and colleagues developed a model including 14 SRL strategies, such as reviewing information (tests, notes, texts), goal-setting and planning, seeking information, help seeking (peers, teachers, adult), and environmental structuring. These types of strategies overlap with cognitive strategies to some degree, but are distinct in their focus on the ways in which students manage, control, and direct their thinking and behavior in pursuit of some type of goal (Zimmerman, 1989; Zimmerman and Martinez-Pons,

1986). In a simplistic sense, SRL strategies help students overcome various internal and/or external challenges or barriers that may interfere with the learning process.

Although there are many other strategy frameworks presented in the literature, I present a simple, two-category framework in this book: *task-focused strategies* and *SRL-focused strategies*. I acknowledge at the outset that this dual-strategy framework is somewhat simplistic and may not fully capture the nuanced distinctions amongst all strategies and tactics. However, it does serve the overarching purpose of helping you recognize that different strategies can serve distinct yet equally important roles as students attempt to complete learning activities in your classroom.

● ● ● ● ●

Task-Focused Strategies

I define *task-focused strategies* as mental processes (ways of thinking) or actions that directly relate to acquiring information or performing a specific academic activity, such as reading a textbook, writing an essay, or conducting a science investigation. As the name implies, task strategies are primarily focused on learning or completing a specific learning activity. For example, suppose Michael's teacher, Mr. Jones, asks his class to write a persuasive essay as an assignment (see Tales of the Student – 3.3). To write this essay, Michael uses a research-based writing strategy called TREE (Topic sentence, Reasons for their position, Explanation for each reason, and Ending or wrapping up the essay) that Mr. Jones taught to the class (Harris, Graham & Santangelo, 2013). The purpose of this strategy is to focus student attention and to guide their thinking about the various components of writing an effective persuasive essay. Thus, the TREE writing strategy would be an example of a task-focused strategy because it directs students' thinking and actions towards the task of writing.

Tales of the Student – 3.3 Michael

Michael really likes his English Language Arts teacher, Mr. Jones, because he frequently speaks to the class about the importance of "being strategic" when they write. Over the course of the past few months, Michael has not only learned about the importance of writing strategies (i.e., tactics on how to brainstorm, to draft a paragraph, and to proofread), he has recently begun to think about almost every procedure he uses in school as a type of strategy. For example, he recognizes that his daily planner is a type of strategy to help manage his time. His tutor has also helped him realize that making certain self-statements when bored or tired is a strategy for motivating himself. Michael also had been very reluctant to ask for help when he was confused. However, because of the openness of his teacher and some helpful suggestions from his tutor regarding how best to seek out help, Michael will often bring up his concerns or questions several times a week to his teacher.

It is well beyond the scope of this book to review all task-focused strategies that are relevant to academic success in schools. As a teacher, I suspect you are somewhat knowledgeable about these strategies. For example, when it comes to strategies for enhancing learning and recall, effective approaches tend to include concept mapping, summarization, self-testing, and distributed practice (see Dunlosky et al., 2013 and Nesbit & Adesope, 2006 for a review of effective strategies). In terms of strategies linked to core academic skills, such as reading comprehension, written expression,

Strategies: Tools for Directing the SRL Loop 41

and mathematics problem solving, the most consistent theme to emerge in the literature involves the importance of getting students *actively engaged* with the content and material. For example, in reading, students often benefit from using strategies like making predictions, relating text information to personal knowledge, monitoring comprehension, and summarizing information after reading (Pressley & Harris, 2008).

As I noted in the example with Michael, the use of writing strategies, such as TREE, are beneficial because they guide students' thinking about the essential aspects of writing a quality essay. These types of strategies get students focused on how they approach and execute the task of writing. Task-focused strategies for mathematics problem-solving adhere to the same basic premise; that is, get students actively using, practicing, and refining how they engage in the mathematics problem-solving process. For example, many effective strategies in mathematics, such as Montague's SolveIT program, guide student thinking about how best to represent the problem, plan solutions, perform calculations and operations, and monitor and check one's work (Montague, Enders, & Dietz, 2014; Fuchs et al., 2003). In sum, regardless of the specific subject matter or content area, task-focused strategies are useful in that they direct students' attention and thinking to the process of performing relevant activities and academic skills.

● ● ● ● ●

SRL-Focused Strategies

Being successful in school requires more than possessing strong academic skills and proficiency in using task-focused strategies. Depending on the complexity and challenges of an assignment or project, students will also need to effectively manage their time, motivate themselves when bored, or structure an appropriate learning environment when practicing their academic skills. That is, they need to deploy *SRL-focused strategies*.

Core Concept 3.2

To develop students' strategic skills, expose them to *a range of strategies* and then provide them with *structured practice opportunities* to use and refine those strategies.

Let's take a look back to the Michael example (see Tales of the Student – 3.3). Although part of his strategic approach related specifically to the act of writing, he realized over time that he also needed to use strategies to manage other aspects of his life. For example, to organize his time he began the writing process three days before the due date (time management strategy) and found a quiet place at home to write the essay (environmental structuring strategy). Because Michael is often not as motivated to do his work at night, he has learned to use self-control strategies, such as self-talk ("Keep going. You only have a little more to go") and self-reinforcement (i.e., rewards himself with 15 minutes of free play on his iPad after finishing a key part of the writing process) to motivate himself. These three SRL-focused strategies (i.e., time management, environmental structuring, and self-control strategies) differ from the TREE strategy in that they facilitate or set the stage for Michael to write a high-quality essay, but they do not specifically pertain to writing skills per se.

In short, I define SRL-focused strategies in this book as purposeful, intentional actions and processes designed to influence student thoughts, behavior, and affect, which support or create opportunities for students to use task-focused strategies. SRL

Table 3.1 Examples and description of SRL-focused strategies

SRL strategies	Description
Help seeking	Procedures to obtain assistance from others when encountering challenge or difficulty on a learning activity (asking a teacher, parent, friend for help)
Seeking information	Procedures to obtain information about a learning activity from non-social sources (textbooks, internet, etc.)
Planning	Procedures to direct the sequence and timing of behaviors to complete a learning activity (e.g., time management, outlines)
Monitoring/keeping records	Procedures to track or to record behaviors, thoughts, or performance (e.g., self-monitoring forms, checklists)
Self-evaluation	Procedures to evaluate the quality of learning, progress or improvement, or assignment completion (e.g., self-testing or quizzing)
Self-motivation	Procedures to enhance motivation for completing learning activities (e.g., self-consequences, positive, self-talk).
Attention-focusing	Procedures to help focus or direct attention to a given learning activity
Environmental structuring	Procedures to structure learning contexts or settings that enhance and optimize learning

Sources: Dunlosky, Rawson, Marsh, Nathan, & Willingham, 2013; Wolters, 2011; Zimmerman & Martinez-Pons, 1986.

strategies may directly influence learning or information acquisition at times, but their primary function is to help students manage, direct, and adapt their task-related thoughts and behaviors. Further, whereas task-focused strategies tend to be specific to an academic skill or learning activity, SRL-focused strategies can be applied to virtually any learning activity. I summarize a variety of SRL-focused strategies in Table 3.1. To think more about how the word "strategic" operates in your classrooms, please complete Reflect and Connect exercise 3.1.

Core Concept 3.3

Task strategies reflect procedures that directly influence student learning or performance on an academic activity, whereas *SRL strategies* enable students to manage and control their thoughts, feelings, actions, and learning contexts as they perform that activity.

Reflect and Connect – 3.1 Conceptions of a Strategy

- Based on concepts you have read so far in this chapter, has your conception of a strategy changed? How so?

- Suppose I came into your classroom and asked your students, "To what extent does your teacher discuss and teach you about strategies to complete your assignments and projects?" What do you think most of your students would say?

Ways to Cultivate "Thinking in the Language of Strategies"

If you thought of yourself as a chef who was interested in creating a couple dozen "strategic learners," you would need to follow a basic three-step recipe: (1) foster student knowledge of task-focused and SRL-focused strategies; (2) provide multiple opportunities for students to think about and use those strategies, and (3) enhance student motivation or desire to want to use the strategies. Given that I have already addressed student motivation in Chapter 2, I focus my attention here on the things you can do to help your students to think about and use *task-focused* and *SRL-focused* strategies during task completion. I present five general guidelines to help you accomplish this objective:

- Make a commitment to TALK IN THE LANGUAGE OF STRATEGIES.
- Model and provide sufficient opportunities for student to practice using strategies.
- Identify the relevant strategies for different learning activities.
- Get students to think about strategies before, during, and after a learning activity.
- Expand the size and quality of your students' "strategy tool box."

Guideline #1: Talk in the Language of Strategies

During my professional interactions with educators, I have learned that the term, *strategy*, is often not a focal point of classroom discourse. Obviously, most teachers provide students instruction about procedures for learning or performing academic skills – that is they often provide some type of strategy instruction. However, the extent to which teachers label these methods and procedures as strategies appears to be less of a focus. From my perspective, a critical first step in getting students to **THINK** IN THE LANGUAGE OF STRATEGIES is to make sure that you frequently and consistently **TALK** IN THE LANGUAGE OF STRATEGIES. Thus, whether you show students how to use the TREE strategy to write a persuasive essay, to utilize a set of procedures for completing a proof in geometry class, or to follow a process for conducting a science investigation, it is important to not only explicitly talk about these procedures, but to label them as types of strategies for completing a specific task.

Steven Graham and Karen Harris are renowned scholars who developed the Self-Regulated Strategy Development intervention program to help students improve their writing skills (Graham & Harris, 2009). As part of this intervention program, students learn to use writing strategies that are represented by "catchy" and memorable acronyms (e.g., POW (Pick, Organize, Write); TREE (Topic, Reasons, Explain, Ending); C-SPACE (Characters, Setting, Purpose, Action, Conclusion, Emotions). Having students associate a simple strategy phrase with a specific set of procedures is important because it enhances recall and prompts them to use procedures that are linked to the target activity (see Tales of the Teacher – 3.1).

Tales of the Teacher – 3.1 Mr. Jones

One of the reasons Michael really likes his English Language Arts teacher, Mr. Jones, is because he gets students excited about "being strategic" when they write. He consistently uses the word "strategy" when teaching about the writing process. For example, when teaching the class about the TREE strategy several weeks ago, Mr. Jones first talked about the purpose and relevance of the strategy for improving student writing. He then acted as a cognitive coping model when demonstrating the strategy; that is, he showed the students how to use the strategy while overtly sharing his thoughts and reactions when using it. He also intentionally made a few mistakes and acted confused when using the strategy, so that his students could observe how to brainstorm about overcoming challenges and confusion when using the strategy.

Mr. Jones also had his students practice using the writing strategies during class. He provided feedback to them about their writing but he also had them work together and share feedback in small groups. Although Michael did not initially understand what Mr. Jones meant by things like "being strategic" or "viewing writing as a process," over time Michael began to view writing as, "how I should approach and think about writing" and "making sure that I follow the process and think about how well I am using the strategies." Having this insight provided Michael with a motivational boost because he now believes that he can learn anything in school as long as he knows the correct strategy – that is, his self-efficacy increased!

Most students will not naturally use strategic language to label the procedures you teach in class. However, by regularly using "strategy labels" when discussing these procedures, you can increase the frequency with which your students think about strategies and can greatly enhance the quality of communication between you and your students.

•••••

Guideline #2: Practice, Practice, Practice

Although Guideline #1 is a key step in the strategy development process, simply talking about strategies with your students is not enough. They will often need explicit instruction and structured opportunities to practice using strategies in authentic situations. Many researchers advocate using a multi-step process when teaching students to use strategies (Gettinger & Seibert, 2002; Pape, Bell, & Yetkin-Ozdemir, 2013; Zimmerman, 2000):

- Explain and model the strategy.
- Provide practice opportunities with feedback.
- Facilitate practice opportunities outside of school (e.g., homework assignment).
- Encourage application of strategies across contexts and classes.

Since a key theme in this chapter is getting students to think about strategies as they learn, I focus exclusively on the first two steps of this process. To begin, it is important to explain the purposes and rationale of the strategy and then demonstrate (i.e., model) how to use the strategy (see Tales of the Teacher – 3.1). Mr. Jones modeled how to use the TREE strategy by talking out loud as he used it. That is, he led the students through the process of developing a topic for the persuasive essay, generating reasons for his argument, and so forth. By sharing his actual thoughts, Mr. Jones enabled his students to observe an effective way to think and react during writing. Mr. Jones also likes to use coping modeling procedures (i.e., model how to use a strategy, but also make and correct mistakes). That is, he intentionally gets "stuck" when using the strategy and then models how to overcome the confusion or problem. This type of modeling is important because it mirrors the experiences that most students encounter when first attempting to use strategies.

Although modeling is a fundamental aspect to the strategy development process, students also need frequent and structured opportunities to practice. Multiple practice formats can be utilized (i.e., homework assignment, completing worksheets in class, small group activities in class), but the most critical ingredient involves providing students with *guided practice* – structured opportunities to use or apply strategies while receiving immediate feedback. That is, most students need to "see" and then "do." While some students will be able to learn how to use strategies after a couple of modeling and practice sessions, many of them will need repeated practice opportunities. Therefore, do not become frustrated when several of your students do not quickly apply and use strategies that you teach them, particularly when the strategies involve complex or multi-step procedures.

Getting students to the point where they routinely use strategies is more of a marathon than a sprint. In fact, it requires a commitment on the part of the teacher and the student. I am sure most of you would agree that most teachers have very little free time during the school day and tend to be overworked in general. Further, due to limited resources or lack of exposure to task-focused or SRL-focused strategies, teachers cannot not bear sole or even primary responsibility for teaching all of the potential strategies that students might need to know. These challenges aside, I very much believe that all teachers can influence students' strategic actions by:

- Increasing the frequency with which they use strategy language in the classroom.
- Modeling how to use the strategies that they want or need students to learn.
- Giving students some structured opportunities to practice using the strategies.

● ● ● ● ●

Guideline #3: Link Learning Activities and Strategies

You will notice throughout this book that I continuously encourage you to identify and think about the specific learning activities, projects, or assignments that are central to your class. My repeated focus on *learning activities* is intentional because I want you to understand the important link that exists between the nature and demands of these activities and how you need to teach SRL and strategic skills. For example, suppose on Tuesday, Michael was asked to read a chapter in a novel for Language Arts and to complete a mathematics worksheet for his homework. The specific strategies needed to perform well on these two tasks would be quite distinct. For the reading task, Michael may use prediction and summarization strategies, whereas for the mathematics problems, he would likely utilize tactics such as drawing pictures to conceptualize the problem and using a systemic approach to check his calculations.

Because learning activities can also vary in complexity and scope, the set of strategies that students may use across situations and contexts will also vary. In short, the more complex or time intensive an activity, the greater likelihood that students will need to use multiple SRL strategies to manage their thoughts and behaviors. Consider the distinction

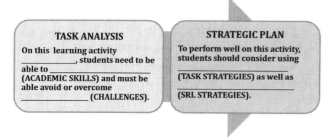

Figure 3.1 Linking task analysis and task strategies before learning

between Johanna completing a mathematics worksheet (five calculus problems) during class and engaging in test preparation activities for a unit test in mathematics. To perform the relatively straightforward task of completing the mathematics worksheet, Johanna would need to focus on correctly using mathematics problem-solving tactics or strategies. While it is true that she may also need to use SRL strategies to help her focus her attention or to ask for help if confused (e.g., attention focusing, help seeking), the primary demands of this activity can be addressed with task-focused strategies. On the other hand, because the test preparation activity is much more time intensive, broader in scope, and complex than the worksheet assignment, Johanna will probably need to enlist a broader array of strategies. In addition to using specific mathematics-focused strategies, Johanna would likely need to adequately manage her time, organize her course study materials, and create a quiet place to study at home.

It is important to remember that as a teacher, you are the content expert and the "designer" of the learning activities used in your courses; thus, you should have an intricate knowledge of those activities along with the strategies (task-focused or SRL-focused) needed to complete them. To help you make this connection between the nature and demands of class assignments and relevant strategies, consider using the instructional prompt presented in Figure 3.1.

Engaging in this type of *learning activity analysis* is important because it naturally prompts you to generate ideas about strategies that are most relevant to excelling on that activity (see Chapter 4 to explore task analysis in greater depth). It might take you a little while before you get the hang of using this prompt, but just remember this ... *if YOU are not able to identify the relevant strategies linked to a learning activity, imagine how difficult this task will be for your students.*

Core Concept 3.4

A key step in enhancing the quality of students' *strategic behaviors* is to increase their awareness of the demands, challenges, and requirements of that activity.

Guideline #4: Thinking Strategically Before, During, and After

Before reading about Guideline #4, please read and complete Reflect and Connect exercise 3.2.

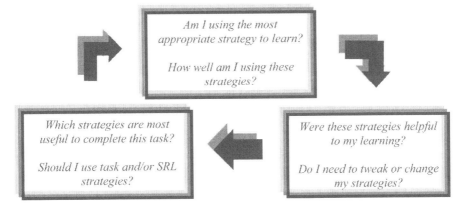

Figure 3.2 Questions to guide strategic thinking during a learning activity

---

Reflect and Connect – 3.2 Extent of Students' Strategic Thinking

Identify a core learning activity that your students complete as part of your class.

- In your opinion, to what extent do your students think about strategies BEFORE attempting that learning activity, DURING completion of that activity, and AFTER completing that activity?

I suspect most of you teach some strategies to your students as a natural part of instruction. However, the issue I raised in Reflect and Connect exercise 3.2 addresses whether you get your students to THINK IN THE LANGUAGE OF STRATEGIES during all phases of task completion (before, during, and after; see Chapter 1). Strategic learners do not simply plan or decide to use strategies every so often. They think about strategies all the time—as they *approach*, *complete*, and *reflect* on the assignments, tests, or projects that they complete. Why is thinking about strategies in a cyclical way important? Well, think about it for a second. If you know that certain strategies are instrumental to students performing well on a given activity, doesn't it make sense to get your students thinking about and using those strategies during all phases of task completion? In Figure 3.2, I present a series of questions that teachers can use to prompt students to THINK IN THE LANGUAGE OF STRATEGIES before, during, and after completing a learning activity.

Guideline #5: Developing a Repertoire of Strategies

Research has demonstrated the effectiveness and power of task-focused and SRL-focused strategies. However, most experts would assert that effective regulators never simply rely on a single strategy to learn in all contexts and situations. In a review of learning strategies used across different academic skills, Pressley and Harris (2008) noted that good writers "engage in purposeful and active self-direction of the processes and skills underlying writing, and like good readers, use a repertoire of strategies" (p. 84). Another prominent researcher in the area of strategic learning, Claire Weinstein, agreed. "Students need a repertoire of learning approaches, strategies, and methods that they can use and adapt to a variety of academic as well as everyday learning situations" (Weinstein & Acee, 2013, p. 206). Thus, as a teacher, it is important for you to remember that teaching students an array of strategies will enable them to more easily and flexibly adapt and change their strategic approach to the assignments, projects, and activities you use as part of your class.

> **Core Concept 3.5**
>
> Teachers can empower students to overcome the challenges they experience in school by helping them develop and expand their *strategy toolbox*.

Concluding Thoughts

As a teacher, it is important that you understand the value in getting your students to THINK IN THE LANGUAGE OF STRATEGIES. Strategies encompass the approaches and procedures that students need to use to learn effectively and to complete assignments and projects. From my perspective, teachers can serve as a guide or facilitator in the development of students' strategic skills and behaviors. Although you cannot (and should not) assume sole responsibility for teaching task strategies and SRL strategies, you can help your students identify the most relevant strategies to use for a given learning activity while also encouraging them to focus on strategies throughout the learning process.

At this point, you have completed reading the *Preparing for Your SRL Journey* section of this book. Yay! In addition to providing you with an overview of the *cyclical feedback* framework of SRL (Chapter 1), I identified two essential themes embedded within this framework: *student motivation* (Chapter 2) and *strategic thinking and action* (Chapter 3). Although these initial chapters were not as "applied" as subsequent chapters, they are critical because they provide the foundation or set the stage for the remaining chapters.

In the next section, *Digging a Little Bit Deeper* (Chapters 4–7), I provide practical tips and recommendations that you can use to infuse SRL principles (task analysis, goal-setting, self-monitoring, feedback, self-reflection) into your classroom lesson plans and learning activities. Collectively, the four chapters in that section are designed to unpack the cyclical feedback loop so that you can clearly see how different SRL processes are naturally intertwined with classroom activities.

References

Butler, D. L., Schnellert, L., & Perry, N. E. (2017). *Developing self-regulating learners*. Upper Saddle River, NJ: Pearson Education.

Cleary, T. J., Velardi, B., & Schnaidman, B. (2017). Effects of the Self-Regulated Learning Empowerment Program on middle school students' strategic skills, self-efficacy, and mathematics achievement. *Journal of School Psychology, 64*, 28–42.

Dunlosky, J., Rawson, K., Marsh, E., Nathan, M., & Willingham, D. (2013). Improving students' learning with effective learning techniques: Promising directions from cognitive and educational psychology. *Psychological Science in the Public Interest, 14*(1), 4–58.

Fuchs, L. S., Fuchs, D., Prentice, K., Burch, M., Hamlett, C. L., Owen, R., & Schroeter, K. (2003). Enhancing third-grade students' mathematical problem solving with self-regulated learning strategies. *Journal of Educational Psychology, 95*(2), 306–315.

Gettinger, M., & Seibert, J. K. (2002). Contributions of study skills to academic competence. *School Psychology Review, 31*(3), 350–365.

Graham, S., & Harris, K. R. (2009). Almost 30 years of writing research: Making sense of it all with the Wrath of Khan. *Learning Disabilities Research and Practice, 24,* 58–68.

Harris, K. R., Graham, S., & Santangelo, T. (2013). Self-regulated strategies development in writing: Development, implementation, and intervention. In H. Bembenutty, T. J. Cleary, and A. Kitsantas (Eds.), *Applications of self-regulated learning across disciplines: A tribute to Barry J. Zimmerman* (pp. 59–87). Charlotte, NC: Information Age Publishing.

Montague, M., Enders, C., & Dietz, S. (2014). Effects of cognitive strategy instruction on math problem solving of middle school students with learning disabilities. *Learning Disability Quarterly, 34,* 262–272.

Nesbit, J. C., & Adesope, O. O. (2006). Learning with concept and knowledge maps: A meta-analysis. *Review of Educational Research, 76*(3), 413–448.

Pape, S. J., Bell, C. V., & Yetkin-Ozdemir, I. E. (2013). Sequencing components of mathematics lessons to maximize development of self-regulation: Theory, practice, and intervention. In H. Bembenutty, T. J. Cleary, and A. Kitsantas (Eds.), *Applications of self-regulated learning across diverse disciplines: A tribute to Barry J. Zimmerman* (pp. 29–58). Charlotte, NC: Information Age Publishing.

Pressley, M., & Harris, K. R. (2008). Cognitive strategy instruction: From basic research to classroom application. *Journal of Education, 189,* 77–94.

Weinstein, C. E., & Acee, T. W. (2013). Helping college students become more strategic and self-regulated learners. In H. Bembenutty, T. J. Cleary, and A. Kitsantas (Eds.), *Applications of self-regulated learning across disciplines: A tribute to Barry J. Zimmerman* (pp. 197–236). Charlotte, NC: Information Age Publishing.

Weinstein, C. E., & Mayer, R. E. (1986). The teaching of learning strategies. In M. Wittrock (Ed.), *Handbook of research on teaching* (3rd ed., pp. 315–327). New York: Macmillan.

Wolters, C. A. (2011). Regulation of motivation: Contextual and social aspects. *Teachers College Record, 113,* 265–283.

Zimmerman, B. J. (1989). A social cognitive view of self-regulated academic learning. *Journal of Educational Psychology, 81,* 329–339.

Zimmerman, B. J. (2000). Attaining self-regulation: A social-cognitive perspective. In M. Boekaerts, P. Pintrich, & M. Zeidner (Eds.), *Self-regulation: Theory, research, and applications* (pp. 13–39). Orlando, FL: Academic Press.

Zimmerman, B. J., & Martinez-Pons, M. (1986). Development of a structured interview for assessing student use of self-regulated learning strategies. *American Educational Research Journal, 23,* 614–628.

Section II

Digging a Little Bit Deeper

4

Forethought: Setting the Stage for Learning

Before anything else, preparation is the key to success.

—Alexander Graham Bell

 Chapter Snapshot

In this chapter, I introduce three concepts that are linked to the forethought phase of the cyclical feedback loop: *task analysis*, *goal-setting*, and *planning*. These three processes are important to SRL development because they "set the stage" for learning. Using case scenarios and illustrations, I convey the meaning and importance of these processes and discuss how teacher can integrate them into classroom activities and discourse.

Reader Reflection – 4.1 Thinking Ahead and Planning

Similar to Reader Reflection exercise 3.1, think about a learning activity that is a key component of your class. How often do you get your students to reflect on the following types of questions *before* they begin that activity:

- What do I need to know about the activity to do well?
  _____
  _____

- How should I approach this learning activity?
  _____
  _____

- What am I trying to accomplish in completing this activity?
  _____
  _____

Introduction

Throughout your career as an educator, you probably have come across students who exhibited exceptional forethought skills – those who plan ahead, ask many questions about assignments or tests, and continuously think about the most effective ways to learn or complete their work. The unfortunate reality, however, is that a large percentage of K-12 students do not approach their schoolwork in this intentional, mindful way.

SRL researchers distinguish between *reactive* versus *proactive* learners (Zimmerman, 2000). Reactive learners tend to engage in learning activities without much preparatory thinking or planning. They do not think too deeply about the requirements of a learning activity (*task analysis*), nor do they develop a clear sense of the things they are trying to accomplish (*goal-setting*) or how they will accomplish them (*strategic planning*; see Tales of the Student – 4.1 Tanya). This fairly mindless and non-strategic approach to learning is problematic for several reasons. Reactive learners tend to wait for results or "signs of struggle" before attempting to figure out what or how they should be performing an activity. In some sense, reactive learners are like planes on autopilot. They travel without much thought until they encounter major forms of turbulence. It is during these moments of danger that students finally attempt to take control of the plane so that it does not crash. From a regulatory perspective, it is much more effective (and safe!) to create a flight plan and to gather all relevant information that could affect the flight (weather conditions, fuel for the plane, final destination, etc.) *before* leaving the runway and taking off.

Tales of the Student – 4.1 Tanya

On Tuesday, Tanya's mathematics teachers, Ms. Martinez, informed the class that they were going to have a unit exam on Friday. Upon hearing about this test, Tanya became nervous because she had performed poorly on her last few exams. Due to her struggles, Tanya was feeling more and more like a disappointment to both her parents and teachers. For the upcoming exam, Tanya attempted to motivate herself by stating, "This time I am really going to focus … I want to get a B+ or an A." Although Tanya dutifully completed her mathematics homework assignments on Tuesday and Wednesday of that week, she did not think a lot about the test until Thursday evening. To prepare for the exam, Tanya decided to look at a few homework assignments that were in her binder and re-read some notes that her teacher distributed to the class. As Tanya studied, she thought to herself, "I hope I am looking at the problems that will appear on the test. Oh well, there is nothing I can do about it now. I just have to stay calm and confident like my tutor says."

Because reactive learners also display vague or unclear goals ("To do my best" or "To do well") they will often struggle to make accurate judgments about their learning progress and are likely to rely on using social comparisons to make evaluative judgments (i.e., "How did I do when compared to my peers?"). Although normative comparisons can provide useful information, they naturally lead students to think about grades and other performance outcomes in terms of their intelligence ("I am dumb" or "I am smart"). As I discuss in several chapters throughout this book, when students struggle in school and evaluate their performance relative to intelligence or "unchangeable" factors, they are likely to exhibit negative motivational reactions and continued underachievement (see Tales of the Student – 4.2 – Peter). In this book, I advocate that teachers help students use goals ("I almost reached my goal") or prior performance ("I did better than my last test") as the standards to evaluate performance (see Chapter 7).

Tales of the Student – 4.2 Peter

Peter thinks school is boring and, at times, does not see the point in devoting a lot of time to something that will not help him in his life. Further, he has recently formed a musical band with a few of his friends because of his interest in music and playing the guitar. When talking to his mathematics teacher, Ms. Maino, about his experiences in the band Peter said, "I love my band. Playing guitar is one of the few things that I am really good at and I want to be a great musician." As the conversation shifted back to his schoolwork, Peter noted, "I do not do as well as other students and I am tired of feeling like I don't measure up. In response to his teacher's questions about his academic goals, Peter indicated, "I don't know. I never really set any goals for school. I just try to get by. I probably won't go to college, so what is the point in trying?" Though Peter said these things to his teacher, on some level he wanted to do better. However, because he constantly felt that he was stupid and less intelligent than his classmates, he wanted to avoid school altogether.

A final problem with reactive thinking is that it leads to a "trial and error" approach to learning. Rather than thinking ahead about the best approach to learn, reactive learners like Tanya, try to come up with quick fixes and short-term solutions to their learning challenges. Although they will occasionally stumble upon a good idea regarding how best to learn, their performance tends to be highly inconsistent and uneven. To help you to think more deeply about the meaning of forethought processes, please complete Reflect and Connect exercise 4.1.

Reflect and Connect – 4.1 Understanding Forethought

Re-read Tales of the Student – 4.1. As noted in the scenario, Tanya is a student who exhibits poor forethought skills.

- In your opinion, which behaviors or thought processes suggest that Tanya exhibits poor forethought?

  _____

  _____

- If Tanya was one of your students, what would you do to help her?

  _____

  _____

A key premise of this chapter is that students need to hone and sharpen their forethought skills (the thoughts and actions that occur *before* a learning activity) in order to engage in effective SRL. Forethought skills includes *task analysis/interpretation, strategic planning,* and *goal-setting.* Collectively, these SRL processes initiate a chain reaction of regulatory thinking and action involving the use of task-focused and SRL-focused strategies (Chapter 3), monitoring behavior and learning (Chapter 6), and evaluating the quality of learning (Chapter 7).

> **Core Concept 4.1**
>
> Getting students to *think ahead* and *plan* is not a waste of time ... it sets the tone and lays the foundation for how students think about and approach learning activities.

Forethought Skills – Charting the Regulatory Path

Similar to an earlier comment made about reactive learners, students who struggle in school are often like a plane rumbling down the runway with a half-empty tank of gas and its navigational system turned off. Although the plane may stay airborne for a little while, it will likely not arrive at the anticipated destination. Eventually, the pilot will need to radio in to air-traffic control for assistance or, like many students in today's schools, simply hope for the best. From an academic lens, students with poor forethought skills will often:

- display a poor understanding of what is expected, needed, or required to perform a given activity (an *understanding of activity* issue)
- begin the activity without making a plan about how to complete the activity (a *strategy planning* issue)
- display a vague sense of what they are trying to attain/accomplish (a *goal* issue)
- resist completing the activity (a *motivational* issue).

It is important to underscore that these forethought skills are not traits or fixed aspects of students' personalities (see Figure 4.1). They collectively represent a set of skills and processes that can be improved through instruction, coaching, and practice. Further, forethought skills do not operate in isolation; they intersect and complement each other in important and reciprocal ways.

Figure 4.1 Key components of forethought thinking

Forethought: Setting the Stage for Learning   57

Core Concept 4.2

Forethought represents a set of task analysis, goal-setting, and planning skills as well as the motivation or desire to perform these skills.

Task Analysis: What Are Students Being Asked to Do?

One of the most important things that students can ask themselves upon receiving an assignment is, "What am I being asked to do?" It sounds like such a simple thing, but most students do not deeply analyze the key components and features of your assignments. As I illustrated with Tanya (see Tales of the Student – 4.1), when students' task analysis skills are underdeveloped, they will struggle to approach learning activities in a strategic and purposeful manner.

Task analysis is fundamental to reading, mathematics, writing, and many other types of learning situations (Butler & Cartier, 2004; Zimmerman, 2000). Deborah Butler, a notable scholar in SRL instructional practices, underscored the value of task analysis. She writes, "In sum, we suggest that task interpretation sets learning in motion and establishes direction for learning. As such, students' adopting the habit of interpreting tasks is foundational to their successful performance" (Butler & Cartier, 2004, p. 1743). To help educators better understand how to think about the learning activities they assign students, Butler and Cartier (2004) developed a model of task analysis that addressed three core features: *purposes, components,* and *structure.*

Task purpose simply involves what the learning activity is designed to get students to do or experience. For example, when writing a persuasive essay, the purpose is to develop an argument or persuade a reader about one's position for a particular topic. Conversely, the purpose of studying for a biology exam might be to develop a conceptual understanding of the skeletal system and to build one's vocabulary of key terms.

Task components involve the key processes that are linked to successful task completion. Thus, in terms of solving algebra word problems, the components involve how to represent the problem using a picture or number line, to translate that model into a numerical equation, and then to solve and check work (Pressley & Harris, 2008).

Finally, *task structure* involves the format, features, or elements of a learning activity that are important when performing that activity. An example of task structure for reading involves the type of text (narrative and expository), while for studying and test preparation it could pertain to the format of test questions or the nature of course materials one uses to study.

Approaching Task Analysis in the Classroom

There are many things that teachers can do to enhance the quality of students' task analysis skills. Building off Butler's model and the supporting empirical literature, I present a three-step process that teachers can follow to promote students' task analysis skills: *enhancing understanding, enhancing perceived value,* and *providing structured practice opportunities* (see Figure 4.2).

58 Forethought: Setting the Stage for Learning

| Help develop a clear understanding of the purposes, components, and structure of learning activities | Communicate that task analysis is valuable and important | Provide structured opportunities to practice breaking down features of a learning actiivty |

Figure 4.2 Sequence of teacher practices to promote task analysis

Step 1: Enhancing understanding of learning activities

Before delving into the first step of this task analysis instructional process, I would like you to complete Reflect and Connect exercise 4.2.

Reflect and Connect – 4.2 Dimensions of Task Analysis

Think back to one of the learning activities you have been reflecting on throughout this book. As you think about that activity, please look at the *Task Analysis* worksheet (see Figure 4.3) and attempt to answer the three questions on that worksheet.

* How easily were you able to answer these questions?

  _____

  _____

* Suppose you gave students the Task Analysis worksheet to complete. How easily do you think they could complete this form? What does this tell you?

  _____

  _____

| What is the purpose of the activity? What do I want students to get out of it? | What are the important processes or steps needed to perform well? | What is the format, features, or characteristics of the activity that students need to know? |

Figure 4.3 Teacher version of a task analysis worksheet

1. What is the primary objective of this activity? (**TASK PURPOSE**)
2. What is the primary thing I should learn during this activity? (**TASK PURPOSE**)
3. Is there a correct or best process to follow when doing this activity? (**TASK COMPONENT**)
4. Is there any aspect of this activity that will be challenging for me? (**TASK COMPONENT**)
5. What are the key parts of the assignment that I need to be aware of? (**TASK STRUCTURE**)
6. Do I have all of the necessary materials to perform the activity? (**TASK STRUCTURE**)

Figure 4.4 Instructional prompt for task analysis

One useful strategy to facilitate student understanding of a learning activity is to engage them in a structured, classroom-based discussion about task analysis. For example, suppose Ms. Maino asked her 9th grade students to complete a mathematics worksheet of problems covered in class over the past month. Ms. Maino divided the class into groups of four to five students (each group was a blend of high and low-achieving students) and asked them to deliberate about different questions across the three task analysis dimensions (task purpose, task component, task structure; see Figure 4.4). After about 5 minutes of small group conversation, Ms. Maino had her students share their answers with the larger group. She validated appropriate student responses, cleared up any misconceptions, and provided additional feedback and information, as needed. In approximately 10 minutes, Ms. Maino was able to actively engage students in task analysis and helped to ensure that everyone was on the same page regarding the assignment.

Step 2: Communicate the value and importance of task analysis

Getting your students to engage in task analysis will not always be an easy thing to do. Part of the problem is that it requires student effort and motivation. As you introduce this process, you will be much more successful in getting buy-in from students if you simultaneously target their motivation beliefs. Let me illustrate how I integrate task analysis and motivation prompts as part of the Self-Regulation Empowerment Program (SREP) intervention used with middle and high school students (Cleary & Platten, 2013; Cleary, Velardi, & Schnaidman, 2017). During the first couple of sessions of SREP, the SRL coaches strategically use analogies or persuasive case scenarios to help students understand the relevance and value of task analysis. These case scenarios are designed to be personally relevant, interesting, and hopefully somewhat enjoyable for students. One scenario that I frequently use involves the principle of "scouting" in a sports context. See below for an excerpt of this activity:

"Have any of you ever played a sport? Which ones?" The SRL coach briefly engages students in a discussion about their participation in sports. "For many team sports, coaches have a lot of responsibilities. One of the most important things they have to do is to "scout" teams that they are going to play. Who can tell me what this means – to "scout" another team?" Have students provide answers and help them to see that scouting involves learning about the other team. "Why do coaches do this?" Engage students in a brief discussion and then say, "To scout another team is important because it helps a coach figure out what types of plays the other teams run, who the best players are, and perhaps what types of defensive or offensive strategies they use during games. So the coach needs to gather information that he or she can use to best prepare and practice with his/her team in order to win the next game" (Cleary, 2014). The SRL coach then relates the concept of scouting to the academic task of interest for the intervention group (e.g., test preparation). Students learn that task analysis for test preparation is akin to "scouting" the test (Cleary, 2014).

I have used other scenarios or topics, such as cooking a meal or going on a family vacation, to engage students in conversations about the importance and relevance of thinking ahead and planning. There are countless other scenarios that can be used, but make sure that the scenarios:

- are appealing, personally relevant, and interesting to students
- convey the importance of "thinking ahead," identifying challenges, and selecting the key strategies needed to perform well.

Step 3: Structured opportunities to practice task analysis

After students begin to understand the meaning of task analysis and its value to learning, they will benefit greatly from structured opportunities to practice their task analysis skills. Most students do not possess an adequate schema (a mental template or script) for task analysis; thus, they will often need practical, easy-to-follow guidelines or prompts to stimulate this type of thinking. Consider the following example of Ms. Johnson, who is Peter's high school science teacher (see Tales of the Teacher – 4.1). Ms. Johnson is preparing to teach a two-week unit on cellular reproduction that will culminate with an exam. To help students become more "proactive" in their approach to test preparation, Ms. Johnson gives students a *Test Preparation* worksheet that they can use to "scout" the next test (see Figure 4.5; Cleary, 2014). This worksheet prompts students to identify and organize information about the essential components and structure of the test preparation activity.

Tales of the Teacher – 4.1 Ms. Johnson

To help Peter and his classmates engage in task analysis, Ms. Johnson gives them about 5 minutes during class a couple of times each week to work collaboratively on a Test Preparation worksheet (Figure 4.5). She permits students to work in small groups to share ideas, to ask questions of each other, and/or to seek out assistance as needed. Ms. Johnson also walks around the room during the brief activity to remind her students about the overall purpose of this "scouting" procedure, to reinforce its value and meaningfulness, and to clarify any misconceptions or challenges that students experience. By getting students to think ahead and to generate their own responses to questions on this form, Ms. Johnson is nurturing students' motivation (autonomy, perceived value, self-efficacy) as well as planting important seeds about becoming more proactive in their learning – that is, students who think ahead (rather than waiting to the last minute), identify key requirements of an assignment, and actively attempt to seek out help or assistance when confused.

What assignments/quizzes/ other work that you completed in this unit will be on the next exam?	What are the major concepts/"big ideas"/key terms that you think will be on the next test?	What topics/ideas/concepts in this unit are challenging for you to learn?
• _____ • _____ • _____ • _____ • _____	• _____ • _____ • _____ • _____ • _____	• _____ • _____ • _____ • _____ • _____

What things prevent you from completing your work?	What WAS the format of the last test?	What WILL be the format of the next test?
☐ I often feel unmotivated to study ☐ I have trouble remembering facts ☐ I do not know how to ask for help ☐ I struggle to take good notes in class ☐ I forget my study materials at school ☐ I do not have enough time to study ☐ I get distracted by others ☐ I do not understand class lectures	☐ Multiple choice ☐ True/False ☐ Diagrams/models ☐ Short answer ☐ Essay ☐ Solving problems ☐ Other _____	☐ Multiple choice ☐ True/False ☐ Diagrams/modes ☐ Short answer ☐ Essay ☐ Solving problems ☐ Other _____

Figure 4.5 Example of a test preparation worksheet

The *Test Preparation* worksheet can help Peter and his classmates approach test preparation in a more effective way because it gets them to:

- become more aware of the *content/information* that may appear on the test
- identify the key *challenges* they are experiencing when learning the topic
- identify the *format* or *structure* of the upcoming test.

For Peter, by proactively figuring out that the next test will involve multiple choice questions, short answer essays, and diagrams, he naturally recognized the need to ask Ms. Johnson some questions and to begin thinking about how he might need to study for each type of question. Further, by "scouting" the test, Peter realized that his study approach should go beyond memorizing facts and key terms. He elected to incorporate other tactics, such as writing out answers to potential essay questions and labeling blank diagrams of cells to self-assess his knowledge in this area. Now that you have been introduced to task analysis, what are your thoughts about this regulatory process (see Reflect and Connect exercise 4.3).

Reflect and Connect – 4.3 Importance of Task Analysis

Think back to the learning activity you identified in Reflect and Connect exercise 4.2 and then answer the follow question.

- Are there ways to tweak or change Figure 4.5 so that it effectively addresses task analysis for this activity?

_____

_____

Core Concept 4.3

Teaching students to "scout" assignments, projects, and tests can help them develop a more accurate *understanding* of these activities and the *plans* needed to complete them.

Setting Goals Prior to Learning

A goal is generally defined as the aim or object of one's actions. It represents something that one hopes to attain — the desired result of performing some activity (Locke & Latham, 2002). There is much research showing that goals exert important influences on student motivation and regulatory behaviors (Locke & Latham, 2002; Schunk, Meece, & Pintrich, 2014; Zimmerman, 2008). Of particular importance to this chapter, is that goals will often prompt students to think about the specific, task-related behaviors that are needed to help them become successful.

Consider the case of Michael (see Tales of the Student – 4.3) and his Language Arts teacher, Mr. Jones. Because Michael was committed to his goal of getting a B+ on his writing assignments, he began to exhibit a variety of behaviors that reflected adaptive motivation. Michael *chose to* follow his teacher's advice of looking at exemplar essays written by former students because he wanted to see what "good writing" looked like. Michael also began to focus more of his *attention* on how he approached his writing (e.g., making an outline and plan) across all types of homework assignments and doubled the amount of time (*effort*) he typically spent on writing at home. Finally, even though Michael was disappointed that his essay grades after setting his goal were below his own expectations (C– and a C), his desire to achieve that goal led him to *persist* by examining the shortcomings of his last two essays and then refining these areas for future essays.

Tales of the Student – 4.3 Michael

Michael was earning C's on writing assignments in his Language Arts class. He wanted to become a better writer and began talking to his Language Arts teacher, Mr. Jones, about how to do this. Mr. Jones communicated two things. First, he told Michael that it was important for him to set a goal for himself – that is, the type of grade Michael wants to attain and one that is realistic. Mr. Jones also reminded Michael about focusing on the general writing process (pre-drafting, drafting, revision, final proofreading) along with the specific writing tactics taught in class for writing persuasive and other types of essays. Because Michael decided that he wanted to get at least a B+ on all of his writing assignments (his goal), he immediately recognized the value and importance of the strategies taught by Mr. Jones. He also thought that it would be a good idea to practice using some of these strategies for writing assessments in other classes. As an additional part of his plan, Michael spontaneously thought that it would be a good idea to create a quiet writing space at home. Because he struggles to write when there are too many distractions, he thought creating this space would be an effective and more efficient way to improve his writing skills. Although Michael still earned C's on his first two assignments, he kept trying because he valued his goal.

It is important to emphasize, however, that getting students to set goals does not automatically cause them to become highly motivated. Students often will need a teacher to nudge or push them in this direction. As I discuss in other chapters in this book, the types of beliefs that students possess (e.g., self-efficacy, growth mindset, interest, value; Chapter 2), as well as the nature and the types of judgments they make following performance (e.g., attributions; Chapter 7), also have important influences on student motivation.

Core Concept 4.4

Enhancing student motivation involves nurturing their *motivation beliefs and perceptions* (e.g., self-efficacy, autonomy support) as well as the *goals* they set for themselves.

Properties and Features of Goals

Although establishing a goal seems like a relatively straightforward endeavor, it is actually a very nuanced process. In fact, Zimmerman (2008) identified seven properties of goals that can have differential effects on student behaviors and perceptions. Broadly speaking, adaptive goals tend to be those that are: *specific* (makes self-evaluation more clear), *self-generated* (promotes autonomy and self-efficacy), *congruent with other goals* (reduces internal conflict and dissonance), *organized hierarchically* (helps students see both short-term and long-term goals), *moderately challenging* (helps student evaluate progress), *conscious* (promotes more mindful, purposeful approaches to learning), and *process-oriented* (focuses student attention on task strategies).

It is well beyond the scope of this book to delve into each of these properties. However, let me illustrate some of them using Michael and John, who are classmates in Mr. Jones' 7th grade English Language Arts class. Suppose both students set personal goals for an upcoming writing assignment. Michael decided to set multiple goals. In addition to his *long-term outcome goal* of earning an A on essays at the end of the semester, he created a *short-term outcome* goal of getting at least a B on his next

Table 4.1 Profile of Michael's goals for a writing assignment

Outcome goals: (1) to get a B on his next writing assignment; (2) to obtain a grade of at least a 90 on his writing assignments by the end of the school year.
Process goal: to perform each of the steps of the writing strategies taught in class.

Property of goals	Type of property	Effects on motivation and SRL
Level of specificity (specific vs general)	Specific	Enables Michael to more clearly evaluate progress (engage in self-evaluation).
Hierarchical structure (short-term vs long-term)	Short-term and long-term	Creating both short-term and long-term goals enables Michael to frequently assess progress (short-term) as he pursues a highly-valued long-term goal.
Level of temporal proximity (immediate vs distal)	Proximal (immediate)	The process goal allows Michael to generate immediate feedback *as he writes* the essay.
Level of difficulty (easy vs challenging)	Moderately challenging but attainable	Enables Michael to frequently experience success and personal progress.
Focus (outcome vs process)	Process and outcome	Use of process and outcome goals allows Michael to evaluate writing performance over time (outcome goals) and facilitates THINKING IN THE LANGUAGE OF STRATEGIES (process goals).

Table 4.2 Profile of John's goals for a writing assignment

Outcome goal: to do well
Process goal: none

Property of goals	Type of property	Effects on motivation and SRL
Level of specificity (specific vs general)	General	Makes it challenging to evaluate progress and improvement (difficult to self-evaluate).
Hierarchical structure (short-term vs long-term)	No hierarchy (short-term goals only)	Enables John to evaluate progress on the next writing assignment but does not allow him to judge progress towards some desired end point.
Level of temporal proximity (immediate vs distal)	Distal (somewhat delayed)	Because John's goal only pertains to the outcome *after* writing the essay, he will not receive any feedback about his writing *as he writes* the essay.
Level of difficulty (easy vs challenging)	Unknown (meaning of "to do well" is vague)	May enable John to experience success but its effects on motivation are minimal. John will likely *not* motivate himself to try hard and will not experience much satisfaction.
Focus (outcome vs process)	Outcome	Shifts John's focus to performance or outcomes only. *Does not* prompt him to THINK IN THE LANGUAGE OF STRATEGIES.

writing assignment. Because he values the use of writing strategies, Michael also set a *process goal* of correctly using different writing strategies taught in class as he writes his essays. Conversely, John developed a positive but overly general and narrow *outcome goal*, "To get a good grade." To more clearly understand the distinction between John's and Michael's goals and the link between goals and student reactions, please see Tables 4.1 and 4.2.

> **Core Concept 4.5**
>
> General goals create ambiguity and uncertainty that can lead to confusion. Whenever possible, have students set *specific, clear, and short-term goals*.

After reading through Michael and John's goals, you might need additional guidance about how to encourage students to set appropriate goals. Further, you might have had some questions as you read through Tables 4.1 and 4.2, such as:

- Should students use process rather than outcome goals?
- Are multiple goals always better than a single goal?
- Should short-term goals be emphasized over long-term goals?

For some of these issues, the research is clear. For example, specific goals are superior to general goals ("To do my best"; "To get better at taking tests"). Specific goals enable students to more accurately and meaningfully evaluate performance ("How well I am doing?"; see Chapter 7). When considering John's vague, ambiguous goal ("To get a good grade"), can he realistically determine whether he ever reaches that goal? Further, what does "good" even mean?

When determining the beneficial aspects of other goal properties, however, the answers are not as clear-cut. Consider the distinction between *outcome goals* and *process goals*. Outcome goals pertain to the level of performance that one hopes to attain, whereas process goals focus on students' use of strategies or the procedures when completing an activity. As a general rule of thumb, process goals are often more desirable, particularly when students struggle or when they are first learning a task. Process goals get students to THINK IN THE LANGUAGE OF STRATEGIES. For example, by developing a process goal of correctly following the steps of the writing strategy taught in class, Michael naturally began to focus his attention and efforts on the process of writing. Isn't this what all teachers want? That is, to have their students think about and actually use the strategies they teach during class.

However, research shows that *both* outcome goals and process goals can have beneficial effects on learning (Zimmerman & Kitsantas, 1999; Zimmerman, Kitsantas, & Cleary, 2000); thus, it is certainly acceptable to encourage students to use both. However, just be careful not to introduce outcome goals too quickly when students first learn a skill. Getting students to focus on outcomes before they master a skill or strategy will shift their attention away from the strategy or process – the very thing students need to focus on to perform well

> **Core Concept 4.6**
>
> Helping students set process goals is another way in which teachers can get students to *THINK IN THE LANGUAGE OF STRATEGIES.*

The distinction between short-term goals and long-term goals is also an important one. Research clearly supports the effectiveness of short-terms goals because they allow students to evaluate progress on a more frequent basis. For example, suppose Michael set a long-term goal of attaining an A on his writing assignments by the end of the semester. This long-term goal is important because it will help to keep Michael's "eye on the prize" or to see the "big picture." However, because this goal is distal in nature (it probably will not be attained for several months) it does not help Michael evaluate progress in the short term. Thus, by supplementing his long-term goal with a set of less stringent yet more proximal outcomes to attain (i.e., a B on his next assignment, then a B+, etc.), he has created a feedback mechanism for tracking progress towards getting the desired A in the course.

Devising a Task-Specific Strategic Plan

Once students have developed a better understanding of the key characteristics and features of a learning activity (task analysis) and have a clear sense of what they are trying to accomplish (goal-setting), they are now in prime position to create the roadmap or strategic plan to perform well on that activity. To get yourself thinking about this next component of forethought, go to Reflect and Connect exercise 4.4.

Reflect and Connect – 4.4 Creating a Strategic Roadmap

Think back to the learning activity identified for REFLECT AND CONNECT 4.2 and 4.3. Please answer the following questions:

- Do you ever talk to your students about how they can effectively complete that learning activity?

  _____

  _____

- If yes, what do you say? How do you teach them to plan?

  _____

  _____

Helping Students Develop a Strategic Roadmap to Success

Having students develop an effective strategic plan depends on several factors. Students need to understand the demands and requirements of the activity (task analysis; Chapter 4) and should possess some knowledge of SRL-focused and task-focused strategies (Chapter 3). They also need to be motivated (at least on some level) to develop the plan (Chapter 2). Although I have previously addressed these three factors, I have not yet addressed how teachers can guide their students in *practicing* planning skills.

Planning Guideline #1: Link Task Demands to Planning Activities

In the previous section on task analysis, I discussed how Peter's use of the *Test Preparation* worksheet enabled him to think more strategically and purposefully about his approach to science test preparation. It is important to emphasize, however, that strategic planning may vary greatly depending on the nature of the assignment or project. Consider two activities that were assigned to Peter. Suppose Peter and his classmates in 9th grade English Language Arts were asked to complete a book report. The assignment was due in six weeks and involved many different parts. The students had to first read the book and then provide a detailed overview and analysis of some key story elements. Because the project was due in six weeks, Peter and his classmates needed to manage their time, organize all materials needed to complete the assignment, and sustain their motivation and focus over time. Due to the complexity of this assignment, students needed to integrate a variety of task-focused strategies (e.g., writing strategies, following the outline provided by his teacher) and SRL-focused strategies (e.g., time management, organization, and self-motivation tactics).

Conversely, suppose Peter's mathematics teacher informed the class that she was giving them a new homework assignment (a sheet of ten word problems) that was due the following day. Because the complexity of completing a homework assignment is much simpler and more narrow in scope than the six-week book report, the nature of Peter's strategic plan for the math assignment would be much less detailed and comprehensive. Thus, a key principle to remember is that teachers do not need to require students to engage in formal planning activities for every assignment nor do they need to be overly intensive in their approach to teaching planning skills. I recommend that you first identify all of the activities you assign in your class, then prompt students to develop plans for the most complex and important ones.

● ● ● ● ●

Planning Guideline #2: Give Students Opportunities to Practice Planning

Because planning requires effort and motivation, and is a skill that many students have not adequately developed, it is important for teachers to provide direct guidance, encouragement, and prompting. For example, suppose Mr. Presto, who is a high school calculus teacher, asks his students to engage in strategic planning on a weekly basis. At the end of each week (a Thursday or Friday), he gives students approximately 5 minutes to complete a *Study Plan* worksheet (see Figure 4.6; Cleary, 2014). The purpose of this worksheet is to get students to identify strategies (both task-focused and SRL-focused) that they may want to use when completing calculus homework over the weekend or during the early part of a week. On Tuesday or Wednesday of the following week, Mr. Presto asks students to break up into groups to share their experiences in using the strategies listed on their worksheets. This brief instructional and collaborative exercise affords students the opportunity to practice their planning skills and to refine their strategic thinking through conversation and collaboration.

● ● ● ● ●

Planning Guideline #3: Integrate Planning with Other SRL Processes

When considering how to help your students develop strategic plans, just realize that planning is naturally connected with other SRL processes, such as task analysis, self-monitoring, and self-reflection. For example, a benefit of using the *Study*

Plan worksheet is that it seamlessly integrates multiple regulatory processes (i.e., planning, self-monitoring, and self-evaluation). Students are not only expected to check off the boxes of the different strategies that make up their weekly plans, they are asked to record whether they used the strategies at home and if they encountered specific challenges when using them. Doing things that integrate forethought processes with other aspects of SRL is a key step in getting students to think and act in empowering, cyclical ways. In section III of this book, I expand on this premise of integrating multiple SRL constructs as part of typical classroom instruction and activities.

Date of test _____ Date to begin studying: _____

Where will I study: _____

Most important thing for me to remember and focus on when studying: _____

TASK STRATEGIES	PLAN	TRIED	SRL STRATEGIES	PLAN	TRIED
Mnemonic device	☐	☐	Use strategies to manage time	☐	☐
Concept maps	☐	☐	Use motivation strategies	☐	☐
Self-quizzing	☐	☐	– positive self-talk	☐	☐
Identify question types	☐	☐	– rewards, tangibles	☐	☐
Create timelines of events	☐	☐	Organize my notes & materials	☐	☐
Summarize/re-write notes	☐	☐	Study in a comfortable place	☐	☐
Practice completing figures	☐	☐	Avoid distractions	☐	☐
Practice writing essays	☐	☐	Ask for help as needed	☐	☐
Other: _____	☐	☐	Look up info (textbooks, internet)	☐	☐
Other: _____	☐	☐	Other _____	☐	☐
Other: _____	☐	☐	Other _____	☐	☐

Are there any things that are preventing me from studying or doing my work?

☐ I often feel "unmotivated" to study   ☐ I forget my study materials in school

☐ I have trouble remembering facts   ☐ I do not have enough time to study

☐ I have trouble understanding how concepts work   ☐ I forget to study or do my homework

☐ I take very bad notes in class   ☐ I get distracted by others (phone, texts)

Figure 4.6 Example of study plan worksheet

Core Concept 4.7

It is important to teach SRL processes as a set of *inter-related skills* rather than as separate, discrete skills.

Concluding Thoughts

Forethought thinking and preparation is a critical aspect of the cyclical feedback loop because it sets in motion a series of events that influence the things students do and think about during learning. Given that most students tend to be reactive learners (i.e., they wait for negative results to occur before taking action), it is important for teachers to think about how they can assist students in becoming more purposeful and strategic BEFORE students work on important projects, assignments, or tasks. In practical terms, this means that teachers should attempt to help students clearly and accurately identify:

- the specific requirements of a given activity
- the things they should be trying to accomplish or attain on that activity
- the strategies that are needed to perform well on that activity
- the best approach and plan for deploying these strategies.

References

Butler, D. L., & Cartier, S. C. (2004). Promoting effective task interpretation as an important work habit: A key to successful teaching and learning. *Teachers College Record, 106*(9), 1729–1758. doi:10.1111/j.1467–9620.2004.00403.x.

Cleary, T. J. (2014). *Self-Regulation Empowerment Program (SREP) coaching manual.*

Cleary, T. J., & Platten, P. (2013). Examining the correspondence between self-regulated learning and academic achievement: A case study analysis. *Education Research International.* 13 pages. doi: 10.1155/2013/272560.

Cleary, T. J., Velardi, B., & Schnaidman, B. (2017). Effects of the Self-Regulated Empowerment Program (SREP) on middle school students' strategic skills, self-efficacy, and mathematics achievement. *Journal of School Psychology, 64*, 28–42.

Locke, E. A., & Latham, G. P. (2002). Building a practically useful theory of goal setting and task motivation: A 35-year odyssey. *American Psychologist. 57.* 705–717.

Pressley, M., & Harris, K. R. (2008). Cognitive strategy instruction: From basic research to classroom application. *Journal of Education. 189.* 77–94.

Schunk, D. H., Meece, J. L., & Pintrich, P. R. (2014). *Motivation in education: Theory, research, and applications* (4th ed.). Upper Saddle River, NJ: Pearson Education.

Zimmerman, B. J. (2000). Attaining self-regulation: A social-cognitive perspective. In M. Boekaerts, P. Pintrich, & M. Zeidner (Eds.). *Self-regulation: Theory, research, and applications* (pp. 13–39). Orlando, FL: Academic Press.

Zimmerman, B. J. (2008). Goal setting: A key proactive source of academic self-regulation. In B. J. Zimmerman & D. H. Schunk (Eds.). *Motivation and self-regulated learning: Theory, research, and applications* (pp. 267–296). New York: Lawrence Erlbaum Associates.

Zimmerman, B. J., & Kitsantas, A. (1999). Acquiring writing revision skill: Shifting from process to outcome self-regulatory goals. *Journal of Educational Psychology. 91*(2), 241–250.

Zimmerman, B. J., Kitsantas, A., & Cleary, T. (2000). The role of observation and emulation in the development of athletic self-regulation. *Journal of Educational Psychology. 92*(4), 811–817.

5

Feedback: The Role of the Teacher

Feedback is the breakfast of champions.

—Rick Tate

 Chapter Snapshot

Feedback is the lifeline of a self-regulated learner. Given its importance, I devote the next two chapters to this issue. While Chapter 5 addresses the *role of teacher feedback*, Chapter 6 shifts the focus to *students' use of self-monitoring tactics* to generate their own feedback. In a general sense, teacher feedback and student self-monitoring seek to accomplish the same thing; that is, to provide information that students can use to improve, adapt, and/or enhance their knowledge or skills. In Chapter 5, I address the different levels and types of feedback that teachers can provide students, and offer several suggestions regarding *how* they can provide such feedback to optimize student motivation and SRL.

Reader Reflection – 5.1 Giving Feedback to Students

Identify an activity (e.g., test, project, paper, presentation, etc.) that is a core aspect of your class. With that activity in mind, think of the most recent situation when you provided feedback to your students about their performance.

- What were the primary types of feedback you provided them (e.g., an overall grade, information about specific correct/incorrect answers, verbal praise statement, written comments, etc.)?

  _____
  _____

- Did you have a particular goal in mind when giving this feedback?

  _____
  _____

- How did most of your students respond to this feedback? Do you they ignore it or use it to improve their learning or skills?

_____

_____

Introduction

Whenever I engage teachers in conversations about the feedback they provide students, their responses typically mirror the research literature; that is, much of their feedback involves praise, general encouragement, and/or some type of performance information (e.g., grades; Hattie & Timperley, 2007). While some teachers reveal that they also try to provide feedback regarding *how* students can more effectively complete a learning activity, this type of feedback is much less common. The most interesting part of these conversations, however, occurs when I probe them about how "purposeful" they are when providing feedback and whether their students make good use of that feedback.

Many teachers freely acknowledge that they do not spend a lot of time planning or thinking about the best ways to provide feedback. They tend to emphasize grades and other indicators of performance, such as specific errors and mistakes. The basic rationale is that by helping students identify their mistakes, students will be better prepared to change and improve those areas. What has always impacted me however, is the level of frustration that teachers often express regarding the apathy and ineffective ways in which their students react to and use feedback (see Tales of the Student – 5.1). In this chapter, I hope to alleviate any feelings of frustration or confusion by equipping you with the knowledge and tools needed to provide effective forms of feedback that your students can use to improve their learning.

Tales of the Student – 5.1 Tanya

In Tanya's 5th grade mathematics class, all students are required to complete several homework assignments each week. Tanya's teacher, Ms. Martinez, looks over each of the students' assignments and typically marks the incorrect and correct answers. She also takes the time to write at least one comment to get students thinking about how they completed the problems on the particular assignment. For example, on a recent homework assignment, Ms. Martinez informed Tanya about the number of problems she solved correctly (6/10) but also wrote on her assignment, "For questions 4, 7, and 8, I noticed that you did not use a number line or draw a picture to help you figure out the problem. Did you try to use these strategies? They can be very helpful to avoid some of the mistakes you made." Although this feedback was positive and constructive, Tanya did not benefit from it. She was too upset about her grade of 60% to even consider reviewing the feedback comments. Tanya has failed many tests and thus does not think she can improve anyway.

Definition of Feedback

Let's start out with a relatively brief and straightforward definition of feedback. In a simplistic sense, feedback is information or data about a person's level of understanding, performance, or behavior. In an ideal world, feedback should help people reduce the gap between what they know or are capable of doing relative to some expected level. Effective feedback should also prompt people to continue using strategies that work well and to discard or modify those that are not effective (Brookhart, 2008; Butler & Winne, 1995; Hattie & Timperley, 2007; Shute, 2008). Shute (2008) echoed this point of view, indicating that feedback is "information communicated to the learner that is intended to modify his or her thinking or behavior for the purpose of improving learning" (p. 154).

One goal of this chapter is to help you "self-assess" the ways in which you provide feedback to students. I also hope to increase your understanding of how the specific things you say and write to students can greatly affect their motivation and SRL skills. In a seminal review of feedback in academic contexts, Hattie and Timperley (2007) provided some guidance about how feedback can be linked to adaptive and mal-adaptive student reactions. They noted that effective feedback should enable individuals to answer one or more of the following questions: *"Where am I going?," "How am I going?,"* and *"Where to next?"* These three questions, although quite simple, are important because they mirror aspects of the three-phase SRL feedback loop, particularly the self-reflection component. Thus, feedback has the potential to guide student judgments about their progress towards a goal or other benchmark (*self-evaluation*), the potential causes of their learning progress (*attributions*), and the ways in which they need to adapt or change in order to improve (*adaptive inferences*). I discuss these three self-reflection phase processes in greater detail in Chapter 7.

Core Concept 5.1

Feedback involves information that can:

- enhance student *awareness* of their knowledge and skills
- serve as a catalyst for students to *adapt* their *strategic behaviors*.

Although teacher feedback is clearly one of the critical factors underlying student success, I want you to read this chapter with two qualifying points in mind. First, I recognize that most teachers are under enormous time, logistical, and curriculum-related constraints. Thus, it is not always easy nor is it feasible for teachers to provide high-quality feedback to all of their students. Second, as you read this chapter, you may notice some "shortcomings" regarding the types of feedback you provide students or the ways in which you administer them. Trust me when I say that these perceptions and reactions are quite normal. In fact, I am as guilty as anyone when it comes to not always providing feedback in the most effective way. To benefit from this chapter, I encourage you to *avoid* viewing feedback as a rigid set of "musts" or "shoulds"; instead, view it as an ongoing, reciprocal exchange between you and your students that hopefully nudges them towards a pathway of enhanced self-awareness, self-confidence, and motivation to improve.

74 Feedback: The Role of the Teacher

What Level of Feedback Do You Give Students?

Feedback is widely regarded as a key determinant of student success. In addition to increasing self-awareness about strengths and weaknesses, it can provide clues or hints about how students can improve (Hattie & Timperley, 2007; Shute, 2008). However, there are many different types or levels of feedback that students can receive, with some being more desirable than others. In this section, I review four levels emphasized in Hattie and Timperley's (2007) feedback model (i.e., self, task, process, SRL). To stimulate your own thinking about the feedback you provide students, please go to Reflect and Connect exercise 5.1.

Reflect and Connect – 5.1 Levels of Feedback

Using the specific learning activity that you identified as part of the Reader Reflection activity 5.1, ask yourself, "To what extent does my feedback for this activity direct students' attention towards:

- how smart they think they are?
- their overall performance on the task?
- the approach or process they used to complete the activity?
- how well they managed or directed their behaviors during the activity?"

Shifting Student Attention to Global Aspects of the Self

Feedback at the *self or person level* involves praise or general information, such as "You are such a smart student," "You did better than most of your classmates'," or "You need to do better." Although this is a common level of feedback given by teachers or parents, it is often too vague and broad to be of any real value in helping students improve their skills. While it is obvious that negative self-feedback comments, such as "You are dumb" or "You will never be good at this" are not effective things to say to children and adolescents, there is also a danger in providing self-feedback about positive performance because it can shift student attention to fixed or stable aspects of the self.

Suppose a teacher provided feedback to a high-achieving student that led the student to conclude that she was smart and intelligent. This seems like a good thing to do, right? It might be in the short term because the student will likely feel good about herself. However, because self-feedback tends to be broad and devoid of task-specific information, it does not provide any information about students' specific task-related skills nor does it help them identify the things they can adapt or improve to perform at an even higher level. Of greatest concern is that when students are conditioned to reflect on school performance in terms of general ability or intelligence – regardless of whether they are successful or not – they will often become preoccupied with how smart they are. Thus, when students get into the habit of viewing tests, projects, or assignments as an indicator of their intelligence (and believe that intelligence is "fixed"; see Chapter 2), they are quite vulnerable to exhibiting a high level of anxiety, avoidance, and feelings of helplessness (see Chapter 7 for a more in-depth explanation).

> **Core Concept 5.2**
>
> Avoid giving feedback that prompts students to focus on their overall *ability*, *intelligence*, or other *global* aspects of the self.

Shifting Student Attention to the Learning Task

In the previous section, I emphasized types of feedback to avoid. However, you are probably more interested in learning about feedback messages that can inspire, motivate, and help your students learn in an optimal way. To this end, I address three feedback levels; *task outcome, task process*, and *SRL process*. Research has shown that each of these feedback levels can have positive effects on student functioning. Although each level is unique and distinct, they all share one common feature: *they direct student attention to some aspect of the learning activities you have assigned them.* As I emphasize repeatedly in this book, a key step in applying SRL processes (and feedback in the case of this chapter) to your classroom is to first develop a clear understanding of the learning activities that you assign your students. The next step is to provide feedback that gets students to:

- analyze their performance on that activity (*task outcome feedback*)
- understand the process or way in which they performed the activity (*task process feedback*)
- reflect on the quality of their self-management or regulatory skills during that activity (*SRL feedback*).

Task Outcome Feedback

Task outcome or corrective feedback involves information about students' performance on an assignment or learning activity. This type of feedback may involve things like overall grades on a project or test, information about correct or incorrect responses (e.g., ✓ or ✗ next to a problem), or statements regarding gaps in students' work. Examples of corrective feedback include, "You got 9 out of 10 correct on the quiz"; "You did not provide an explanation of your answer to the mathematics problems"; "I need to see more details to support your arguments in these paragraphs." This category of feedback tends to be most helpful when used to inform students that they misunderstood something rather than they lack knowledge about the topic (Hattie & Timperley, 2007). Please complete Reflect and Connect exercise 5.2 to think further about how you provide outcome feedback in your classrooms.

Reflect and Connect – 5.2 Reactions to Outcome Feedback

- Do you typically provide task outcome feedback to your students? (i.e., grades, indicators of correct/incorrect responses)?

_____

_____

- In your opinion, does this type of feedback help your students in any way? How so?

_____

_____

From an SRL perspective, task outcome feedback is valuable because it enables students to answer the self-evaluation question, *"How did I perform on this learning activity?"* – a key first step of the self-reflection phase process (see Chapter 7). While task outcome feedback can help students evaluate how well they performed and may at times prompt them to analyze why they performed that way, it does not explicitly guide students to think about *how* to improve. To be able to do this, students need information that helps them identify the potential causes of their outcomes (*attributions*) as well as the potential ways to overcome them (*adaptive inferences*). That is, students need ideas and information that will nudge them to think differently about learning or completing an activity in the future.

Core Concept 5.3

Task outcome or corrective feedback is an important *but not sufficient* level of information to get students thinking and acting in cyclical, strategic ways.

Process Feedback

In order for students to become more strategic as they learn in school, they will often need to receive information that speaks to how they approach or complete an activity – something that researchers call *process feedback*. In this section, I differentiate between two levels of process feedback: *task process feedback* and *SRL process feedback*. I define task process feedback in terms of students' use of strategies, procedures, or tactics that are directly linked to specific learning activities. For example, suppose Tanya received a 72 on a recent mathematics exam. After she had a chance to look over the exam, her teacher briefly stated:

> I noticed that you did not circle the key words in the problems nor did you draw pictures to represent the problem. Do you remember how to do these things or do you need some help with that?

and

> Did you simply re-read your notes or did you practice solving problems from the sheet that I handed out before the class?

Although these two feedback statements are relatively simple, they can have quite a profound effect because they direct Tanya's attention to her own behaviors and strategy use rather than to an outcome (e.g., grade). As students gather information about their strategic approach to an activity, they will often begin to reflect on their performance in school relative to these strategies. Why is this so important? As I will discuss in greater detail in Chapter 7, when students develop the habit of reflecting on performance in terms of their strategies or other behaviors, they will naturally begin to focus more on their strategic actions than how smart or capable they think they are. This mindset will help them to more easily re-strategize or tweak their use of strategies when learning in the future.

Core Concept 5.4

Task process feedback can help steer students towards an empowered and motivated pathway of *THINKING IN THE LANGUAGE OF STRATEGIES*.

I have mentioned several times in this book that SRL is a type of process – a sequence of task-related activities whereby students approach an activity with a certain mindset or perspective (forethought), implement strategies and keep track of their performance (performance control), and then analyze how they performed (self-reflection). Because SRL is a process, any feedback that pertains to SRL skills can also be considered a type of process feedback. *SRL process feedback* is distinct from task process feedback, however, because it emphasizes information about how students manage, control, or direct their thoughts and behaviors during task completion. This distinction is similar to the point I raised in Chapter 3 regarding task-focused and SRL-focused strategies. That is, task-focused strategies (as with task process feedback) focus the methods or approaches individuals use to directly learn information or to complete a learning activity. Such strategies might involve using the TREE strategy to write an essay (Graham & Harris, 2009) or a problem-solving strategy to complete algebra word problems (Montague, Enders, & Dietz, 2014). In contrast, SRL-focused strategies (as with SRL feedback) pertains to the methods and approaches that students use to manage their thinking, motivation, and behaviors as they perform a learning activity. Examples of SRL strategies might include time management, motivational self-talk, structuring one's learning environment and seeking out help.

Let's refer back to Tanya to further illustrate this distinction. Suppose Ms. Martinez provided the following feedback statements to Tanya regarding the recent mathematics exam.

> I sometimes get the impression that you don't always know which types of math problems you do well and those that are hard for you. You may want to use this checklist to keep track of the things you get correct and incorrect as you do your work.

and

> I know you are disappointed but I do not think that this grade of 72 and your other recent grades mean that you are unable to do math. I have seen you solve some challenging problems so I know you can do it. I think you struggle at times because you don't always use problem-solving strategies, like drawing a picture or using a number-line strategy, that we talked about in class.

Both of these feedback statements are examples of SRL feedback because they target aspects of the SRL process. The first statement directs Tanya's attention to the importance of *tracking or monitoring* her use of task strategies (see Chapter 6). The focus of the second feedback statement addresses SRL-related information in two ways; it targets Tanya's sense of self-efficacy (see Chapter 2), as well as the types of attributions that she should make following her performance (i.e., her insufficient use of strategies was the reason for her poor performance; see Chapter 7). You may have noticed that the second feedback statement also mentions task-focused strategies (i.e., number line, drawing a picture). Is making statements that concurrently reference both types of process feedback a problem for students? Of course not! In fact, it is often desirable to do so because it helps students understand the importance of regulating their use of task strategies as they learn in school.

To think more about what you have learned so far about feedback, please complete Reflect and Connect exercise 5.3.

Reflect and Connect – 5.3 Reacting to Types of Feedback

- Given that you have learned about different levels of feedback, do you have a more clear sense of the feedback you typically provide students? Which level of feedback do you emphasize the least?

  _____

  _____

- What are your overall reactions to the types and ways in which you provide feedback to your students?

  _____

  _____

From my perspective, task outcome, task process, and SRL feedback are all relevant and important to developing strategic and reflective learners; they simply differ in how and where they direct students' attention. Whereas task outcome feedback gets students to think about performance success or failure (self-evaluation), task process feedback and SRL feedback guide students to think about their behaviors and approaches to learning. Because your feedback can directly influence the nature and focus of students' self-reflective thoughts, be sure to:

- be purposeful in the feedback messages you provide
- provide different levels of feedback to address multiple dimensions of student performance.

Core Concept 5.5

Use feedback as a way to get your students to think about things that YOU want or need them to focus on.

Important Issues About Teacher Feedback

I suspect many of you have some concerns or questions about your role in giving student feedback. It would not surprise me to hear some of you say, *"Well, all of this sounds good on a conceptual or theoretical level. But how realistic is it for me to provide a lot of feedback to students? Also, it is not clear how I am supposed to give students process or SRL feedback when I am not at home with them when they complete their work or when they study. I do not see what they actually do."* These are legitimate and valid concerns. Without fully addressing these issues in this chapter, let me just say that generating feedback for students is a shared responsibility between you and your students. That is, while teachers should provide some feedback, most students possess the capacity to generate their own feedback (see Chapter 6).

To conclude this chapter, I focus on two additional themes about feedback. The first involves principles that teachers should follow when providing feedback to students. For example, should feedback be immediate or delayed? Should the feedback be written down or provided orally? Should it be very detailed or concise? A second general issue pertains to how teachers can enhance the likelihood that students will actually use their feedback. Following one of my recent professional development workshops with a group of elementary and secondary school teachers, one teacher told me, *"I do not know why I even spend time giving them feedback ... they don't even read my comments. I try to help them but most just ignore it."* I address these two critical issues in the following sections.

How Can You Provide Feedback in an Optimal Way?

There is no hard and fast rule regarding how feedback needs to always be delivered. In fact, the optimal way to provide feedback will often vary based on student characteristics (e.g., achievement level, self-efficacy, growth mindset), the situation, or the nature of the learning activity (e.g., challenging vs. easy; short-term vs. long-term).

I do not think I am going out on a limb when stating that most students do not think deeply about or use the feedback you provide them in any meaningful way. I certainly empathize and understand what this feels like. It is quite disappointing and frustrating when you take the time and effort to provide feedback to students, yet they simply ignore or dismiss it. Though frustrating, students' general unresponsiveness to feedback shines a light on an important feedback principle:

> "Effective" feedback does not simply pertain to the levels or types of feedback (self, task outcome, process) or even the ways in which teachers provide information to students; it also involves the extent to which students think about, interpret, and use those feedback messages.

Dylan Wiliam, a noted feedback scholar, aptly captured the importance of the student learner in the feedback process. "What seems odd in retrospect is how long it took psychologists to realize that we cannot understand feedback without thinking about how recipients react to the feedback" (Wiliam, 2012, p. 32).

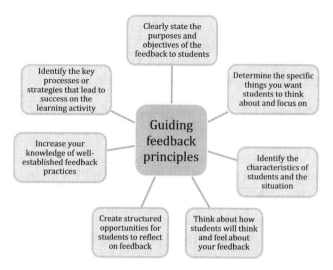

Figure 5.1 General principles for providing feedback to students

Because providing feedback is not always a clear-cut and easy thing to do, I developed a general guide for teachers to use when providing feedback (see Figure 5.1). The primary purpose of this guide is to help you organize your thinking about *what*, *how*, *when*, and *why* you are providing feedback to your students. The feedback guide includes several core principles that are organized into two broad categories; pre-submission and post-submission activities.

Teacher Feedback: Before Students Submit an Assignment

The process of generating feedback *should not* begin at the point when you are actually reviewing and evaluating student work. From my perspective, it is ideal to view feedback as an ongoing sequence of activities that is initiated before students submit a paper, project, or other activity. In the next section, I underscore a few important principles that can help prepare you to provide effective feedback.

Learn About Effective Feedback Practices

One of the simplest things you can do to provide high-quality feedback is to enhance your knowledge of effective feedback practices, both in terms of the levels of feedback (self, task outcome, task process, SRL) as well as the methods for providing that information. The unfortunate reality is that students may not always receive feedback that helps them in any way. Feedback can lack detail and be too narrow in focus (task outcome versus process), or be overly negative or harsh. Consider the case of Michael and his social studies teacher, Ms. Lemme (see Tales of the Student – 5.2). Although Michael is a motivated student who appreciates getting feedback from his teachers, he does not understand her checkmark system and is frustrated by the lack of information and direction she provides.

Tales of the Student – 5.2 Michael

Michael has been struggling to perform consistently in his social studies class this year. Consistent with his long history of reading comprehension difficulties, Michael struggles to complete homework assignments when they involve a lot of reading. Unlike his experiences in English class with Mr. Jones, however, Michael is fairly negative and despondent about his performance in social studies class. Part of the reason for his negative feelings is that his teacher, Ms. Lemme, provides very general and ambiguous feedback. For example, on homework assignments, Ms. Lemme writes either ✓+, ✓, ✓– on the top of the paper. Because there are very few comments on the paper, Michael does not really understand what these check marks mean. Similarly, on exams, Ms. Lemme simply places a line through incorrect responses to multiple-choice problems or indicates the points lost on a short answer/essay question. Although this type of feedback lets Michael know the specific questions that were challenging for him (task outcome feedback), he is often at a loss about what to do about his errors (task process feedback). Of particular frustration for Michael is that following his most recent exam Ms. Lemme told him, "I know you are smart but you have to try harder." This was difficult for Michael to hear because he believes that he was trying hard. He thought to himself that perhaps he just cannot handle the workload in this class.

Understand the Key Components of Your Activities

A second guiding principle is developing a clear understanding of the key components and challenges of your class assignments as well as the strategies needed to successfully complete them. This guideline is particularly important for teachers interested in providing *process* feedback to students. It is very difficult for teachers to provide process-related information unless they think deeply about the learning activities and the typical challenges that students encounter. For example, suppose Ms. Lemme asked her students to write a short paper about the primary factors that led to colonial unrest and discontentment with British rule. She distributed an outline to students that delineated the key requirements of the paper. To prep herself about feedback that she can potentially provide students, Ms. Lemme reflected on the key areas of challenge that students have historically had when completing this assignment. She also identified a few critical strategies that she knows are effective in getting students to write a high-quality essay. Because she had fleshed out and identified the primary components of this writing assignment, she was better positioned to think about and provide feedback about "process-related matters" when reading and evaluating student papers.

Core Concept 5.6

To provide effective *process feedback*, teachers need to understand the components and challenges of a given learning activity as well as the relevant strategies linked to that activity.

Teacher Feedback: After Students Submit an Assignment

Identify Your Purposes and Goals in Providing Feedback

An important factor in getting students to adaptively respond and react to your feedback involves ensuring a match or fit between your feedback and students' expectations of that feedback. Thus, this factor can be broken down into two separate ideas: (a) teacher intentions and goals, and (b) student expectations.

Students may misunderstand your feedback if you do not clearly convey to them *why* you are giving that feedback and how it can help them (Brookhart, 2008; Wiliam, 2012). To the greatest extent possible, when I work with my graduate or undergraduate students, I strive to clearly communicate the purpose of my feedback and offer guidance about how best to perceive and interpret it. As an example, one of the papers I assign in my class is divided into three "mini" papers. The first two minis are ungraded and are designed to promote self-reflection and evaluation of the process that they followed. I tell my students something like,

> I will be providing a lot of written feedback on your papers. The purpose of the feedback is to help you to see how well you followed the overall guidelines of the assignment and to also convey the quality with which you developed and expressed your ideas. Although I will provide some comments that speak to the strengths of the paper, my primary goal is to get you to reflect more deeply about the ways you can more effectively approach the assignment.

Ultimately, there is no way that I can completely control how my students will think about my feedback. In addition, I have to admit that I do not always preface feedback in this way (no one is perfect!). However, by being transparent and proactively setting the foundation for students to think about and reflect on feedback, we as educators can often reduce some of the ambiguity that pervades teacher-student feedback exchanges.

Think About When You Should Provide Feedback

In most situations, students will not use feedback when it is overly complex and detailed and when there is a large delay in receiving the feedback. Consider the case of Mr. Filipo, Johanna's physics teacher (see Tales of the Teacher – 5.1).

Tales of the Teacher – 5.1 Mr. Filipo

Johanna is frustrated with her physics teacher, Mr Filipo. Whenever Johanna and her classmates turn in assignments or take quizzes and tests, Mr. Filipo takes a fairly long time to give feedback. Unbeknownst to Johanna, the reason he takes so long is because he wants to make sure that all students receive enough feedback so that they can improve. Thus, Mr. Filipo tends to write many comments on all of his students' papers. He does not want to demoralize students who struggle, thus, he also makes sure that he writes more positive than negative comments. Although much of his feedback is of high quality (both task and process feedback), Mr. Filipo gets frustrated because he perceives that many of his students, like Johanna, simply "do not care enough to take my feedback seriously." While it is certainly true that some students may not take the feedback seriously because they are not interested in the feedback, the reality is that Johanna is not one of those students. She is highly motivated and would undoubtedly use the feedback to improve her performance if it was made available to her in a timely way; but because of the long delay, Johanna often disregards its relevance and importance.

The timeliness with which students receive feedback about performance is a logistical and real concern in schools. Because teachers have so much on their plates, such

Consider Student Characteristics

Suppose Ms. Martinez wants to provide task feedback to Tanya (a student who often performs below expectations) and one of her classmates, Joey (a student who performs well in school), regarding a fairly complex class assignment. Should her feedback to both students be the same? Research evidence indicates that, at times, the nature of the feedback should differ based on students' characteristics (Shute, 2008). For example, high achieving students like Joey may benefit more from feedback that provides verification of correctness, includes prompts and hints (suggests what he needs to do), and is somewhat delayed (not given immediately after the task is completed). Conversely, lower-achieving students like Tanya are more likely to benefit from feedback that is immediate, and is both explicit and directive (tells her what she needs to do). Interested readers should consult Shute (2008) for information regarding additional feedback principles.

Identify Student Perceptions and Beliefs

As mentioned previously, there may be times when students ignore your feedback. It is also possible, however, that teacher feedback can have a negative influence on student motivation. In looking back to the scenario with Ms. Lemme and Michael (see Tales of the Student – 5.2), some of her feedback statements were ineffective because they were based on faulty assumptions about Michael. Ms. Lemme told Michael that he needs to try harder in order to perform well. Although this statement was probably well-intentioned (she wanted to encourage and motivate Michael), Ms. Lemme incorrectly assumed that Michael was not trying hard. Because Michael perceived that he was putting forth a lot of effort but then was confronted with the message, "all you need to do is try," he was left to wonder whether he was capable of doing the work.

The above scenario is just one example underscoring the importance of paying attention to the links that naturally exist among student beliefs and perceptions, the learning activities they are asked to complete, and the feedback that teachers provide them. Student self-efficacy or confidence is particularly important in this regard. Consider the case of Tanya. Even though Ms. Martinez often provided high quality process feedback, and did so with grace and sensitivity, Tanya often disregarded this information because she feels incapable of taking action. Thus, teachers need to toe that line between providing information about things that students need to correct or improve while simultaneously conveying that information in a way that fits with student perceptions of competence to perform those things.

I also encourage teachers to proactively think about and analyze the things students may need (in terms of feedback) in order to perform well. Think back to Mr. Filipo and Johanna. Because Mr. Filipo was confused about why his students ignored his feedback, he decided to engage his entire class in conversation about this issue. A few students expressed their frustration about the length of time it takes for them to get feedback as well as the excessive number of comments that he provides them. Many of the students noted that they simply wanted a couple of the most important things to fix so that they can get better grades on the next assignment. These conversations were helpful to Mr. Filipo because it forced him to re-think his approach to providing feedback.

Please note that I am not suggesting that teachers should base their feedback messages entirely on what their students want to hear. However, by not seeking to understand student perceptions and preferences, teachers may unwittingly create a context whereby students ignore or tune out their feedback.

Part of the process of providing effective feedback is to create a climate of "collaborative exchange" whereby students are encouraged to ask questions and to clarify misconceptions while simultaneously feeling reassured and encouraged. Some researchers have referred to this type of exchange as a *feedback dialogue* — an ongoing, reciprocal exchange between feedback provider (teacher) and recipient (student; Nicol & MacFarlane-Dick, 2006). In Chapter 7, I provide specific examples regarding how teachers can use feedback dialogues to engage students in the process of feedback interpretation and analysis.

Core Concept 5.7

When thinking about how to provide feedback to students, be mindful of how they might perceive or interpret it, and whether they understand your intentions in providing it.

Concluding Thoughts

The type of feedback that you provide students has the potential to place them on a pathway of empowered strategic thinking and action. However, this is not an easy thing to do. Some feedback (e.g., process, SRL) is more effective than others (e.g., self). Further, several factors influence the effectiveness of feedback, such as the manner in which teachers deliver feedback as well as the beliefs, perceptions, and characteristics of students receiving the feedback.

As you attempt to provide effective feedback to your students, it is important to keep in mind a few important principles:

- Feedback does not simply flow in one direction (i.e., from teacher to student). It involves a constant exchange of information between you and your students.
- Identify the most important things that you want students to think about as part of a learning activity – then give them feedback about those things.
- Be mindful of your primary goals and objectives for providing feedback to students, and then openly communicate these ideas to your students.

References

Brookhart, S. M. (2008). *How to give effective feedback to your students*. Alexandria, VA: Association for Supervision and Curriculum Development.

Butler, D. L., & Winne, P. H. (1995). Feedback and self-regulated learning: A theoretical synthesis. *Review of Educational Research*, 65(3), 245.

Graham, S., & Harris, K. R. (2009). Almost 30 years of writing research: Making sense of it all with the Wrath of Khan. *Learning Disabilities Research and Practice, 24,* 58–68.

Hattie, J., & Timperley, H. (2007). The power of feedback. *Review of Educational Research, 77*(1), 81–112. doi:10.3102/003465430298487.

Montague, M., Enders, C., & Dietz, S. (2014). Effects of cognitive strategy instruction on math problem solving of middle school students with learning disabilities. *Learning Disability Quarterly, 34,* 262–272.

Nicol, D. J., & MacFarlane-Dick, D. (2006). Formative assessment and self-regulated learning: A model and seven principles of good feedback practice. *Studies in Higher Education, 31*(2), 199–218. doi:10.1080/03075070600572090.

Shute, V. J. (2008). Focus on formative feedback. *Review of Educational Research, 78*(1), 153–189. doi:10.3102/0034654307313795.

Wiliam, D. (2012). Feedback: Part of a system. *Educational Leadership, 70*(1), 31–34.

6

Feedback: Shifting Responsibility to the Student

I think self-awareness is probably the most important thing towards being a champion.
—Billie Jean King

 Chapter Snapshot

In Chapter 5, I made the case that teacher feedback is important because it can help students adapt and improve their learning and performance in school. While this is true, I now discuss how students can also play a role in the feedback generation process via *self-monitoring* tactics. In Chapter 6, I define and explain the core components and benefits of self-monitoring. I then provide examples and case scenarios to illustrate how teachers can infuse monitoring activities as a routine part of classroom activities and assignments.

Reader Reflection – 6.1 Students as Self-Monitors

Think about one or two common learning activities or projects that you assign in your class:

- To what extent do you encourage or help your students monitor how well they perform these activities? Specifically, how do you do this?

- To what extent do you ask students to monitor their actions and/or use of strategies when completing these activities?

Introduction

When I conduct professional development workshops, most teachers agree with the general premise that students often need feedback to improve in school. They also agree that certain types of feedback, such as process and SRL feedback, are critical in promoting student growth. However, I also receive push back at times. Some teachers raise concerns that it is unrealistic to expect them to serve as the sole or primary source of feedback because providing feedback can be very time consuming. Examples of comments that I might hear during a workshop include:

- "I have a lot of content to cover, papers to grade, and so many personalities to manage in my class. It is simply too time intensive and unrealistic to expect teachers to provide high-quality feedback to all students on a continuous basis throughout the school year."
- "I am a middle school teacher. I only see my students for 40–50 minutes a day. I do not have the chance to really 'see' how many of them approach, think about, or reflect on their learning. It is really difficult for me to give good feedback when I do not know what they are doing outside of class."
- "I agree with you that students are often very unaware of what they know and what they don't know … so giving them feedback is really important. But I don't think it is realistic to expect teachers to point out all of these things for students. Shouldn't students figure out how to do some of these things themselves?"

After hearing these types of comments, my response would likely be something like, "Yup. That makes a lot of sense!" or "I understand exactly what you mean!" In short, I wholeheartedly agree that there is no way that teachers can provide students with all the necessary information to help them improve and excel. At some point, students need to generate some of this information on their own; the key thing, however, is that they will need help in doing so.

The central theme of this chapter is that students can supplement teacher feedback by monitoring their own thoughts and actions as they complete classwork and homework. It is my hope that after reading this chapter, you will be able to:

- recognize the benefits of getting your students to self-monitor
- understand the basics of teaching self-monitoring approaches to your students
- infuse self-monitoring procedures as an integral part of core classroom activities.

● ● ● ● ●

Self-Monitoring ... A Pathway to Enhanced Self-Awareness

An important aspect of the SRL cyclical feedback loop is *self-observation* or *self-monitoring* (I use these terms interchangeably). Self-observation represents the internal process through which students gather information about their thoughts, behaviors, and performance. Thus, in a sense, self-monitored information is a type of feedback.

Students have the potential to monitor many different things. They can assess their behaviors (e.g., length of time spent studying, use of a writing strategy), the contextual factors that influence those behaviors (e.g., distractions encountered during studying), and/or performance outcomes (e.g., homework completion, grades on a mathematics test; Zimmerman, 2000). Regardless of the specific things that students may monitor, the process of self-monitoring is important because it can help students generate more information than what teachers could realistically provide.

From my perspective, all students can monitor what they think, do, and feel (at least to some degree). Thus, whether it is Johanna's use of a simple recording form to track areas of challenge during homework (see Tales of the Student – 6.1) or Michael's use of a form to monitor his use of a writing strategy (see Tales of the Student – 6.2), students can learn to generate their own feedback. They just simply need the support and guidance to do so.

Tales of the Student – 6.1 Johanna

Johanna was performing well in almost all of her core academic classes in 11th grade. However, her honors physics class was giving her some difficulty. Apparently, the concepts were more complex than in previous years. The assignments were also longer and more detailed. Despite her struggles at the beginning of the year, Johanna figured out a way to overcome these challenges. Each night that she completed her homework or studied for a quiz or exam, she used a monitoring sheet to write down one or two things that were confusing or difficult. If Johanna could not figure out how to resolve the issue on her own, she brought the monitoring sheet to class the following day to ask her teacher the question. Because Johanna was able to ask her teacher specific questions about her challenges, she was able to develop a better understanding of how to adapt and improve. Her grades began to improve and her confidence about overcoming these challenges soared. Johanna was also particularly satisfied and proud of the fact that *she was the one* who figured out why she was struggling. It was as if she was a mini-detective and was searching on her own for clues about why she struggled.

Tales of the Student – 6.2 Michael

Michael was performing fairly well on his writing assignments in his English Language Arts class – he typically received B's on these assignments during the most recent quarter. These grades reflected much improvement over his performance on similar assignments in previous marking periods (C's and D's). Michael was particularly appreciative of Mr. Jones' requirement that students graph all of their grades on writing assignments. By graphing his grades, Michael was able to easily determine whether he was improving or not. Even though Michael made some progress, he wondered whether he could do even better. Because Michael's brother was an A student, Michael wanted to perform like him. One day, Michael approached Mr. Jones to ask him about how he might improve his writing. Mr. Jones reminded Michael that he occasionally forgets to use some of the writing strategies taught in class. He handed Michael a checklist that listed all of the key steps in the writing strategy taught in class (see Figure 6.1). Mr. Jones told Michael that it could be helpful if he rated how well he thinks he performed each step of the strategy. Mr. Jones also left an open space next to each step of the writing strategy so that Michael had the opportunity to write a question or comment when confused.

Core Concept 6.1

Encouraging students to monitor their thinking and actions during learning can provide them with clues about *how* to improve their performance.

TREE strategy	How well did I do? 2=outstanding 1 = OK 0 = not well	Was anything about this assignment difficult for me?
Topic		
Reasons		
Explanation		
Ending		

Figure 6.1 Example of self-monitoring form for writing activities

● ● ● ● ●

Benefits of Self-Monitoring

Although teaching students to self-monitor in your class may take some time and effort (your own and your students), the benefits far outweigh the costs. First, engaging students in the self-monitoring process is one of the most effective ways to reduce some of the burden or workload that teachers experience. Most teachers want to provide individualized and meaningful feedback to their students, but there is only so much time in a day. Further, when students track their own actions or levels of productivity, they will gain access to more *specific* and *nuanced* information than what teachers could typically provide them. For example, because Michael recorded his use of a writing strategy as well as the challenges that he encountered, he generated individualized and process-oriented feedback – types of information that Mr. Jones often could not provide his students.

Engaging students in self-monitoring can also have motivational benefits. In many instances, self-monitoring promotes student autonomy and instills a sense of personal responsibility and competency. As discussed in Chapter 2, when students experience greater freedom and autonomy, they will often feel empowered to give the necessary level of effort to improve. This premise was illustrated in the case of Johanna (see Tales of the Student – 6.1). Because Johanna made the choice to keep track of the difficulties encountered when completing her work (rather than her teacher), she felt that the information was more relevant and personally meaningful. In addition, because she became more successful over time in identifying her primary areas of challenge and discovered that *her own actions* led to repeated "demonstrated success" experiences, her self-efficacy began to improve.

Self-monitoring can also enhance student motivation because it provides a more private space from which students can reflect on their behaviors and grades. When teachers provide constructive (or non-constructive) feedback about a poor performance on an assignment, students may worry that their teachers "think I'm stupid" or that "I am not as smart as other kids." Thus, self-monitoring can help minimize the intensity and weight of negative emotional reactions, such as embarrassment and shame, that students may experience following failure.

Finally, self-monitoring practices naturally increase student self-awareness about their strengths and weaknesses. Thus, self-monitoring is a wonderful technique to convey "performance reality" to students and to provide them with clues about how to improve. Peter is fairly typical of students with whom I have worked as part of my intervention work (see Tales of the Student – 6.3; Cleary, Velardi, & Schnaidman, 2017); that is, students who perform below expectations and who are largely unaware of why they struggle and what they need to do to improve. In reviewing Peter's situation, it is clear that he overestimated his knowledge, skill level, and overall competence. This phenomenon, which researchers refer to as calibration accuracy (Bol et al., 2005), is a function of poor monitoring and self-awareness. When students are poorly calibrated, they will often misjudge the level of effort and motivation that they need for a learning activity. For example, because Peter believed that he was performing fairly well in school (poor monitoring and self-assessment skills), he felt that he did not need to spend a lot of time studying or preparing for his most recent exams.

Tales of the Student – 6.3 Peter

Peter was performing inconsistently in school. Although he was beginning to do a better job of completing homework assignments, his performance on major tests or assignments ranged from C's to D's. At a recent meeting, Mr. Gebbia, who was Peter's guidance counselor, asked Peter how he was doing in school. Much to Mr. Gebbia's surprise, Peter responded that things were going really well and that he probably should be receiving B's in most of his classes for the 3rd quarter. Based on Mr. Gebbia's interactions with Michael's team of teachers, he knew Peter's 3rd quarter science test grades were 68, 71, 85, 64, and 70; grades that were much different than what Peter thought he was earning. As one might expect, when the report card grades were distributed, Peter was disappointed to see that he earned grades of C or lower in all of his academic subjects, except for a B in social studies. During a weekly meeting with Mr. Gebbia, Peter was somewhat embarrassed, stating, "I can't believe I got those grades. I thought I was improving." When asked by Mr. Gebbia why he did not do as well as he thought he would, Peter responded, "I have no idea. I think my grade in science is wrong. I was doing really well on tests this quarter." Apparently, Peter focused on his one grade of 85 as a sign that he was performing well in science and seemed to disregard his other test grades.

What Types of Things Should I Ask Students to Self-Monitor?

At this point, I hope you are beginning to understand that getting students to self-monitor can have many positive effects on both students and yourself. But let's dig deeper and try to identify the *types of things* that you may want your students to monitor. To get yourself thinking about this issue, go to Reflect and Connect exercise 6.1 and answer the questions.

Reflect and Connect – 6.1 What to Self-Monitor?

- Think about one of the core learning activities you assign in your class. If there was one thing that you really want students to keep track of or monitor as they complete that activity, what would it be? Why?

  _____

  _____

- How would you get students to monitor that area?

  _____

  _____

Although there are countless things that students can be asked to monitor as they learn, I want to address two broad categories: **performance outcomes** (i.e., work completion, productivity, and grades) and **task behaviors or process** (i.e., strategy use, academic-related behaviors; Cleary et al., 2017; Harris et al., 2005). Getting students to monitor outcomes and their strategic behaviors are important, albeit for different reasons.

Monitoring Outcomes

A performance outcome is a broad term that could involve a course or test grade (percent or number correct), a score generated from a scoring rubric (1–4), level of productivity or work completion (i.e., homework completion rates) or some other indicator of performance. Although getting students to monitor outcomes is fairly straightforward, this activity can have substantial benefits for students. One benefit is that it helps students separate "fact from fiction". As an example, consider Michael's English Language Arts teacher, Mr. Jones, and his decision to ask students to graph their essay grades throughout the entire year (see Tales of the Student – 6.2). After several assignments and class discussions in the early part of the school year, Mr. Jones realized that many of his students were largely unaware of the quality of their actual writing skills and performance. Because Mr. Jones felt that getting his students to develop a more accurate perception of reality (in terms of their writing skills) was a key first step in getting them to improve their writing, he instituted the graphing procedure as a routine aspect of many classroom activities.

Graphing is a highly desirable way to get students to monitor outcomes. In addition to research showing that graphing can promote students' learning gains (Calhoon & Fuchs, 2003; Kitsantas & Zimmerman, 2006), graphs represent powerful visual displays of information that help students identify trends or patterns in their learning over time. In recent years, graphing procedures have been included as part of different SRL academic intervention programs (Cleary et al., 2017; Fuchs et al., 2003; Graham & Harris, 2009).

Similar to the effects of outcome feedback, self-monitored performance outcomes will also enable students to answer the self-evaluation question, "How well did I do?". However, as I will highlight in Chapter 7, self-evaluation is just one part of adaptive self-reflection. Students will need a different type of information to help them reflect in more meaningful and strategic ways (see Reflect and Connect exercise 6.2).

Reflect and Connect – 6.2 Monitoring Process

- Do you ever ask your students to monitor or keep track of the procedures or strategies they use when completing an activity?

  _____

  _____

- Do you think getting your students to track their behaviors or strategies is valuable? Why or why not?

  _____

  _____

Monitoring Processes

In my experience, most students do not routinely keep track of their performance outcomes in any structured or systematic way. Unfortunately, even fewer students think about and monitor their *behaviors* or *use of strategies* when learning. As I keep mentioning in this book, getting students to THINK IN THE LANGUAGE OF STRATEGIES is a key aspect of SRL instruction. That is, it is vital to get students to become more in-tune with how they approach learning activities. Because teachers may not have the time nor the knowledge of students' strategic behaviors to provide sufficient *process-related feedback*, helping students to monitor these processes becomes that much more important.

The benefits of monitoring strategy use were underscored with Michael in his English Language Arts class. In addition to graphing his essay grades, Michael learned how to monitor two process components of his writing; use of a writing strategy taught in class and the challenges he encountered during writing. By tracking his use of the writing strategy at home, Michael generated information that could guide his attempts to seek out help from Mr. Jones during class or to help Michael personally identify the skills he needs to improve. Another potential benefit of Michael recording his strategic behaviors is that Mr. Jones can review the monitoring sheet and then provide additional feedback for Michael. Thus, in some sense, self-monitored information and teacher feedback can inform and complement each other.

> **Core Concept 6.2**
>
> If you want to enhance students' strategic approach to learning:
>
> - give them process-oriented feedback, or
> - have them monitor their behaviors and use of strategies.

What Can I Do to Promote Self-Monitoring in My Students?

Several things can get in the way of student's attempts to engage in self-monitoring. Because self-monitoring requires students to expend mental and physical effort, they need to possess some level of motivation. As most of you already know, most kids do not like to do any "extra" work. Students also need to be knowledgeable about when and how to engage in self-monitoring. In the next section, I offer a few recommendations that teachers can use to enhance the frequency and quality of student self-monitoring during classrooms activities and/or assignments.

Recommendation #1: Identify the Most Essential Things to Monitor

Consistent with my recommendations in other chapters, it is critical that teachers first develop a clear and thorough understanding of the *most essential* behaviors, skills, or strategies needed to complete a given learning activity. When teachers possess this level of task knowledge, they will be better able to guide and coach students in their monitoring activities.

It is not feasible, nor is it desirable, to have students keep track of overly complex or comprehensive outcomes or behaviors. The KISS method is a popular acronym that can guide your thinking about the things you ask students to self-monitor. Whether you use this acronym to mean Keep it Simple Stupid, Keep it Simple Silly, or Keep it Simple and Straightforward, the underlying principle is that *simplicity* is the key ingredient to effective self-monitoring. Students are more likely to engage in self-monitoring when the requirements are straightforward and focused rather than complex or time-intensive. Think back to Michael. As you may recall, Mr. Jones encouraged Michael to use a monitoring checklist to keep track of how well he implemented a specific writing strategy taught in class. The form also prompted him to write down any challenges he encountered during each step.

Suppose Mr. Jones created a monitoring form that also required Michael to record his overall experiences when using the strategies, and to write down all of the specific things that he did well when completing each step of the strategy. Although monitoring these other dimensions might be useful, at some point Mr. Jones needs to ask himself, "How much is too much?" If students feel overburdened or are asked to monitor too many things, they will likely resist engaging in these activities.

Core Concept 6.3

DO: Encourage students to monitor the things that are MOST essential or critical for them to succeed on a learning activity. **DON'T:** Encourage students to monitor too many things.

Recommendation #2: Have Students Monitor What They are Capable of Monitoring

I also recommend asking students to only monitor things that they are *capable of monitoring*. Consider Peter, who although struggling in most of his classes, is somewhat unaware of his performance and skill deficits. Peter's mathematics teacher, Ms. Maino, noticed that he was getting certain types of questions wrong. She thought it was important to help Peter become more aware of these trends. If Ms. Maino stated to Peter, "A good strategy to help you figure out how to do better is to keep track of the types of questions you get wrong on the tests", how likely is it that Peter will actually do that?

Without providing some structure to help Peter understand the meaning of "tracking questions" and the different ways to accomplish this (i.e., giving him a monitoring form), it is likely that Peter will not take her advice. As you may recall from Chapter 3, students often need a lot of repetition and practice in using strategies before they use them effectively. This general rule also applies to self-monitoring. Most of your students will need explanations, demonstrations (modeling), as well as prompts to use self-monitoring worksheets or graphs.

Recommendation #3: Make Sure To Target Students' Motivation Beliefs

Self-monitoring is an effortful activity. It is not something that most students naturally do. Thus, it is important for teachers to remember to infuse motivation-enhancing feedback as students learn and practice using self-monitoring tactics. Consider the following exchange between Johanna and her physics teacher, Mr. Filipo, regarding her use of a self-monitoring sheet when studying:

> **Johanna**: Mr. Filipo, I was wondering if I can ask you a few questions about the last exam.
>
> **Mr. Filipo**: Of course … not a problem. What is on your mind?
>
> **Johanna**: (*Johanna took out a self-monitoring sheet on which she listed a few questions*) When I was doing the homework, I was not able to get the correct answer to these two problems no matter what I did.
>
> **Mr. Filipo**: (*He was a little intrigued by the self-monitoring sheet and asked*) What is the sheet that you have there?
>
> **Johanna**: What, this? This is something that I use to remind myself of all of the things that confuse me or that I cannot figure out when I am studying.
>
> **Mr. Filipo**: Wow, that is amazing. The questions you wrote are very specific, which really should help you to remember what the problem was (*efficacy-enhancing*). Also, I am glad to see you doing this type of thing. When you go to college, keeping track of what you do well or not can really help you (*value-enhancing*). I have actually seen some students in college use certain phone apps that can easily track these things. I can show you some of those after school if you are interested (*interest-enhancing*).

This brief exchange illustrates the close connection between teacher behavior and various student SRL processes: *teacher feedback* (things that teachers communicate to students), *student motivation beliefs* (e.g., self-efficacy, interest), and *student use of an SRL-focused strategy* (self-monitoring). That is, teachers can motivate students to engage in self-monitoring by providing feedback statements that:

- enhance students' competency beliefs about self-monitoring (*self-efficacy*)
- make the monitoring activities enjoyable (*task interest*)
- help students understand the value or relevance of self-monitoring (*task value*)
- give students choice about when and how to use self-monitoring (*autonomy*).

Applications of Self-Monitoring in the Classroom

Monitoring Performance Outcomes: A Case Study

As noted in Tales of the Student – 6.3, Peter was struggling in his science class, particularly for unit exams and lab reports. During his weekly meeting with his school counselor, Mr. Gebbia, Peter expressed a high level of frustration with his progress. Peter was particularly upset on that day because in addition to performing poorly on yet another science lab, he was asked by his teacher, Ms. Johnson, to record and graph his lab report score (see Figure 6.2). Before reading about this case in greater detail, please complete Reflect and Connect exercise 6.3.

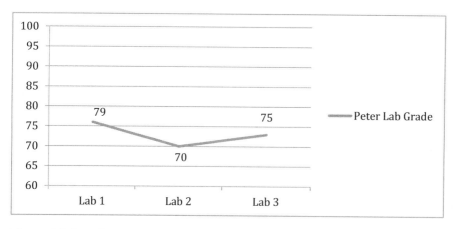

Figure 6.2 Peter's grades on science lab reports

> **Reflect and Connect – 6.3 What Will Peter Think?**
>
> - Take a look at Peter's graph of his last three science lab scores (Figure 6.2). What types of things do you think Peter will think about or reflect on after looking at this graph? In other words, what will he likely conclude regarding his skills and overall competency?
>
> _____
>
> _____

When looking at this graph, Peter shook his head and stated, *"I just can't do this stuff. My teacher is the worst and I have no clue what I am doing. This is just stupid."* This was not the first time Peter expressed negative feelings about science. He frequently blamed his teacher but also felt bad about himself because of his perceived lack of ability. This situation is not uncommon for many students who struggle in school; that is, they reflect on and think about their performance in negative and unproductive ways.

Given Peter's reaction, was it wrong for Ms. Johnson to have her students record their lab grades on the graph, particularly for those students like Peter who struggle? From my perspective, NO it was not. Getting students to become aware of their performance reality (regardless of whether it is positive or negative) is a critical part in helping them to become self-aware, regulated learners. However, teachers do need to consider a few points. First, there is a danger in asking students to *only* record global outcomes, such as grades on projects, tests, or even report card grades. Broad performance indicators often mask specific strengths or areas of mastery that students have attained. In recognizing this fact, Mr. Gebbia felt Peter would benefit from a more nuanced monitoring process. He decided to set up another meeting with Peter to help him keep track of his grades in a different way. In preparation for this meeting, Mr. Gebbia asked Peter to drop off his three prior lab reports. Mr. Gebbia wanted to review them prior to the next meeting. In reviewing these labs, Mr. Gebbia had an idea about how to help Peter gather more informative and meaningful feedback about his lab scores. Mr. Gebbia gave Peter a monitoring form and asked him to complete it (see Table 6.1).

On this monitoring form, Peter was asked to record the number of points earned for each section of the lab report. The primary objective in using this form was to help

Table 6.1 Self-monitoring worksheet for science lab reports

Section of Lab (total points)	Lab #1 points earned	Lab #2 Points earned	Lab #3 Points earned	Points earned/ Total possible points
Experimental procedures (25)	23/25	22/25	23/25	68/75 = 90.7%
Analysis (25)	15/25	13/25	12/25	40/75 = 53.3%
Results (25)	22/25	15/25	19/25	56/75 = 74.6%
Conclusion (15)	10/15	10/15	12/15	32/45 = 71.1%
Format (10)	9/10	10/10	9/10	28/30 = 93.3%
TOTAL	79/100	70/100	75/100	—

Peter identify *patterns* or *trends* in his performance across the different components of the lab. Interestingly, as soon as Peter finished filling out the form, he spontaneously stated, "*I know my overall grade still stinks, but it looks like I am actually doing pretty well on a couple of the sections.*" Mr. Gebbia added to Peter's positive self-reaction by providing self-efficacy-enhancing feedback. "*Look at the last column. It appears that you have actually mastered two of the five key parts to this task, and did OK on the third. But like you just said, the overall grade is not what you want. You now should focus on figuring out the strategies that would best help you improve on the other two sections.*" Peter then smirked and said, "*That is a good point … at least I know what I need to ask my teacher about when I go for extra help today.*"

There are a couple of key take-away messages from this scenario. First, just because Peter got upset about his overall grade does not mean that having him record or graph performance outcomes was inappropriate. In fact, getting him to become more aware of "performance reality" is an important step in the process of improvement. The problem with the original monitoring procedure had more to do with the *level of the outcome* that Peter was asked to monitor. Because Peter was originally asked by his teacher to graph the overall science lab grades rather than the sub-components, it was inevitable that he would interpret his performance in a negative way – that he was not smart and that his teacher was ineffective. However, when Peter used the monitoring form and "discovered" that there was more to his performance on the lab than his overall grade, he began to evaluate the situation differently. In a sense, using the monitoring form shifted his focus from a global, negative type of self-evaluation ("I can't do this") to a more empowering one ("I have mastered some skills but not others"; see Chapter 7 for an elaborated discussion on adaptive self-reflection). As reflected in Peter's comment about knowing what to ask his teacher during extra help, students will often benefit when teachers help them become more cognizant or aware of the fine-grained aspects of their performance.

Core Concept 6.4

Prompting students to monitor *specific* and *fine-grained outcomes* can help them develop a more nuanced understanding of their strengths and weaknesses.

A second take-away theme from the Peter scenario is that engaging in self-monitoring activities enable students to "discover" unique things about their performance and helps them to experience a higher level of autonomy support. Because Peter identified his profile of strengths and weaknesses on the lab report (rather than being told this information by his teacher), he was much more likely to become invested in using that information to improve or change his behaviors. The unfortunate reality in today's schools is that most students are "talked at" most of the time; they are continuously told what to do and reminded about what is expected of them by their parents, teachers, or other adults. By structuring opportunities for students to monitor their own skills and outcomes, teachers can play a key role in helping students take greater ownership, responsibility, and control over their lives!

● ● ● ● ●

Monitoring Performance Processes: A Case Study

In Chapter 5, I noted that outcome feedback, although important in some respects, is not as useful as process feedback for guiding students' attempts to adapt or change their behaviors when not performing well. The basic theme with process feedback is that because it involves information about *how students learn* and/or *how they use task-specific strategies*, it can help them re-strategize their approach to learning. The same logic and reasoning applies to self-monitoring processes or strategies. Getting students to keep track of their behaviors and strategies during learning will help students to THINK IN THE LANGUAGE OF STRATEGIES.

Consider the case of Michael, who was very interested in improving his writing skills and overall performance. As you may recall, Mr. Jones encouraged Michael to use a monitoring form to track his use of a writing strategy when completing assignments at home (see Figure 6.1). Part of the reason why Mr. Jones recommended this monitoring tactic was because Michael did not consistently use all parts of the writing strategy. Thus, he wanted to help Michael become more cognizant of the key "processes" or "strategies" linked to successful writing. This is an example of an exchange between and Michael and Mr. Jones regarding the issue. Mr. Jones stated,

> "Michael, sometimes I get the impression that you do not remember to use all of the steps of the writing strategies that we talked about during class. Here is a worksheet that I would like you to take home with you and use whenever you are writing a persuasive essay for this class (see Figure 6.1). The basic idea is for you to rate yourself on how well you think you did each part of the TREE strategy. A "2" means that you did an outstanding job; a "1" means that you did the part OK; and "0" means that you did not do well on that part. You will probably not use the strategy perfectly and you may get confused at times. That is OK. But if you do get confused about any of the steps, simply write down some of your thoughts in the space to the right. We can then talk about what went well and what was difficult for you."

Interestingly, Mr. Jones and Michael both benefitted from using this monitoring tool. Because the form prompted Michael to focus on the steps of the writing process and to think about the challenges encountered, he naturally began to THINK IN THE LANGUAGE OF STRATEGIES every time he worked on the essay. Getting students to focus on the strategic elements of a learning activity as they practice and learn is a powerful way to help them improve.

Given Michael's goal of becoming a better writer, the monitoring form was also helpful because it helped him keep track of the aspects of the writing process that were challenging for him. Michael used this information to reflect on his own writing but also shared the form with Mr. Jones to obtain even more feedback and support. Mr. Jones welcomed reviewing Michael's self-monitoring worksheet because it shed light on the challenges and difficulties that Michael experienced when writing. Having access to this information helped Mr. Jones engage in more meaningful conversations with Michael about his writing skills and the things that Michael might want to adjust or change in order to improve.

Concluding Thoughts

Self-monitoring and teacher feedback have a very similar purpose – to give students data or information that they can use to adapt and improve their learning. As the previous example with Michael and Mr. Jones illustrated, self-monitoring and teacher feedback are complementary and reciprocal processes. In a metaphorical sense, both of these feedback mechanisms are like a source of oxygen that enables the SRL process to breathe and flourish. Without access to feedback information, the regulatory process will simply wither or go awry.

A unique benefit of self-monitoring relative to teacher feedback, however, is that it not only helps students discover things about themselves as learners, it reduces some of the burden placed on teachers. Self-monitoring also cultivates perceptions of human agency and autonomy. It is when students come to realize that they do not need to depend on others that they can finally take that leap to greater responsibility and ownership of their educational success.

References

Bol, L., Hacker, D. J., O'Shea, P., & Allen, D. (2005). The influence of overt practice, achievement level, and explanatory style on calibration accuracy and performance. *The Journal of Experimental Education, 73,* 269–290.

Calhoon, M. B., & Fuchs, L. S. (2003). The effects of Peer-Assisted Learning Strategies and curriculum-based measurement on the mathematics performance of secondary students with disabilities. *Remedial & Special Education, 24*(4), 235.

Cleary, T. J., Velardi, B., & Schnaidman, B. (2017). Effects of the Self-Regulated Empowerment Program (SREP) on middle school students' strategic skills, self-efficacy, and mathematics achievement. *Journal of School Psychology , 64,* 20–42.

Fuchs, L. S., Fuchs, D., Prentice, K., Burch, M., Hamlett, C. L., Owen, R., & Schroeter, K. (2003). Enhancing third-grade students' mathematical problem solving with self-regulated learning strategies. *Journal of Educational Psychology, 95*(2), 306–315.

Graham, S., & Harris, K. R. (2009). Almost 30 years of writing research: Making sense of it all with the Wrath of Khan. *Learning Disabilities Research and Practice, 24,* 58–68.

Harris, K. R., Friedlander, B. D., Saddler, B., Frizelle, R., & Graham, S. (2005). Self-monitoring of attention versus self-monitoring of academic performance. *The Journal of Special Education, 39(3),* 145–156.

Kitsantas, A., & Zimmerman, B. J. (2006). Enhancing self-regulation of practice: The influence of graphing and self-evaluative standards. *Metacognition and Learning, 1*(3), 201–212. doi:DOI: 10.1007/s11409-006-9000-7.

Zimmerman, B. J. (2000). Attaining self-regulation: A social-cognitive perspective. In M. Boekaerts, P. Pintrich, & M. Zeidner (Eds.), *Self-regulation: Theory, research, and applications* (pp. 13–39). Orlando, FL: Academic Press.

7

Self-Reflection: Making Sense of Feedback

What is the good of experience if you do not reflect?

—Frederick the Great

 Chapter Snapshot

Gathering information or feedback about performance from teachers or through self-monitoring is a vital aspect of the regulatory process, but it is not the end game. From an SRL perspective, the most critical thing is whether students can use this information to evaluate, analyze, and react to their performance in constructive ways. In Chapter 7, I discuss what it means to self-reflect. In addition to using case examples and scenarios to illustrate the reflection process, I discuss several practical, easy-to-implement strategies that teachers can use to promote adaptive self-reflection in the classroom.

Reader Reflection – 7.1 Responding to Moments of Challenge

Think about a recent situation when you wanted to learn how to do something or to perform a particular skill. However, you were not very good at it – at least initially. The skill or activity could involve your role as a teacher or can represent a more a leisurely or "fun" activity (e.g., learning how to dance). The key thing is to make sure that the activity you select was important to you and that you really wanted to do well at it. As you think about this situation, please answer the following questions:

- What *types of thoughts* did you have upon realizing that you were not very good at the activity? (What did you say to yourself?)

  _____

  _____

- What were you feeling at that moment of realization (e.g., anger, shame, anxiety, etc.)?

  _____

  _____

- How did you react after experiencing these thoughts and feelings? (What did you do?)

  _____

  _____

Introduction

A nearly universal experience for school-aged children and adolescents is when teachers return graded tests, projects, papers, or other class assignments. For many students, these situations represent a high-stakes, emotional "moment of truth." During my time as a school-based practitioner, I had numerous opportunities to observe students and their reactions to performance feedback. As one might expect, students who performed well on assignments/tests typically displayed positive affect and reactions, whereas those who struggled exhibited more maladaptive responses. What struck me, however, was the vast differences in the thoughts and behaviors among the lower-achieving students. Whereas some students made light of their struggles by cracking jokes or saying things like, "I really don't care anyway," others, like Tanya (see Tales of the Student – 7.1), displayed a more serious or dejected look on their faces. These latter students would often try to conceal their grades from those sitting around them – such as quickly placing the exam or assignment in their folder or binder (probably to never look at it again) even if the teacher was reviewing it with the class.

Tales of the Student – 7.1 Tanya

Upon returning to school on Monday from a fun and exciting weekend with her cousins, Tanya's good feelings quickly changed as Ms. Martinez returned a unit exam from the previous week. Ms. Martinez told the class, "I was really happy to see improvement in some of your test scores. I know how hard everyone has been working, so keep it up." The class average on the prior exam was an 81, but on the most recent exam, the average was an 85. Unfortunately, Tanya struggled on both of these tests, obtaining a 67 and a 77, respectively. Upon receiving her latest test score, her heart sank. Seeing yet another disappointing grade and realizing that many of her classmates were still performing better than she was, Tanya felt embarrassed and ashamed. From her perspective, her test grade was yet another reminder about how dumb she was in mathematics. She shoved the test in her binder and began ruminating about how bad she was at math. She lamented, "I just can't do this stuff … it is not my thing. I was always bad at math and I probably always will be." When Tanya went home that day, her parents asked her about the test. After talking about how hard the test was, she stated, "My teacher goes too quickly in class. She is not a very good teacher."

During these observations, however, I also learned that not all students who struggle in school think about their grades in a negative way or as a sign that they are "stupid" or incompetent. In fact, some students perceive a less than optimal grade in a somewhat positive way. Consider the case of Michael (see Tales of the Student – 7.2). Although Michael did not attain his personal goal of a B+, he noticed that his grades actually improved from a D to a C+. In his eyes, this level of improvement was a positive thing and he felt satisfied about that. Michael's response pattern is highly distinct from Tanya who, despite demonstrating similar improvement, interpreted her recent test performance as a failure.

Self-Reflection: Making Sense of Feedback 103

> **Tales of the Student – 7.2 Michael**
>
> Michael is a 7th grade middle school student who recently received an essay back from his Language Arts teacher, Mr. Jones. Michael earned a C+ on the paper, which was below his goal of obtaining a B+ on all of his essay assignments. However, because Michael has been earning mostly D's on his writing assignments since the beginning of the year, he interpreted his grade of C+ as a "big improvement" and something that "is getting me closer to my goal." In fact, Michael was particularly excited about his last grade because he began to realize that his efforts in using the writing strategy taught by Mr. Jones was helping him to better understand the aspects of good writing. He thought to himself. "I just need more practice."

Many factors could have led to the distinct performance reactions of Tanya and Michael. At a basic level, student personal beliefs and perceptions are critical determinants of how they react to grades on school assignments, tests, or projects. In this chapter, I detail three critical sub-processes that underlie student reflection: perceptions of the quality of their performance (i.e., *self-evaluation*), perceptions of *why* they performed that way (i.e., *attributions*), and conclusions about *how* to fix or improve the situation (i.e., *adaptive inferences*). Although I have alluded to these concepts in the previous chapters, I now discuss them in detail.

Response to the Reader Reflection Exercise

Before delving into the different aspects of self-reflection, I wanted to provide some commentary about the Readers' Reflection activity presented at the beginning of this chapter. I often use this activity as part of teacher professional development workshops addressing student motivation and SRL because it typically leads to meaningful and insightful discussions with the teachers.

After teachers complete the reflection activity, I ask two or three of them to share their stories or experiences. In many instances, they report their "struggles" as being an intense event, both on a mental and emotional level. For example, at those moments of realization that they were not very competent at the activity, many of them revealed experiencing negative, self-defeating *patterns of thinking* ("I didn't think I could do it ... I felt dumb" or "I just wasn't good enough") and corresponding *negative emotions* (frustration, embarrassment, anger). Several others discussed their maladaptive *behavioral responses*, such as avoiding or disengaging from the activity– at least initially. Although some teachers also noted that they quit or gave up, some expressed that they eventually figured out what to do; that is, they stuck with the activity until they were able to improve. It is at this moment of the conversation that I begin to get at the essential theme or purpose of the activity.

I remind teachers that the majority of them are well-educated, high achieving, and savvy professionals who possess a long history of success, such as graduating from college, possessing an advanced academic degree, and/or getting tenure. Thus, most exhibit a track record of "demonstrated success." Due to these repeated success or mastery experiences, it makes sense they were often able to withstand and overcome some setbacks or failures. The pinnacle of this conversation occurs, however, when I shift the focus back to their students. To paraphrase, I typically say something like:

> "So eventually many of you were able to figure out what you needed to do to improve. But think back to those "moments of truth" when you first encountered struggle and challenge. What did you think about? How did you feel? How did you react? Like many of you have already said, you began to have self-doubts or believed that you were not competent in that skill. Many of you probably felt a little embarrassed and ashamed, and thought about giving up or quitting. Perhaps some of you quit the activity. To be honest, these experiences are normal. Everyone encounters challenge from time to time.
>
> But now, I would like you to think about your students, and, in particular, those who struggle in your class – students who rarely get above a 75 on a test or those who struggle to receive passing grades on most of their writing assignments or science lab reports. Many of these students have struggled for years and thus will not have a strong foundation of 'demonstrated success' (thereby low self-efficacy). Given that all of you, who are quite capable and successful professionals, reported experiencing negative thoughts, emotions, and reactions following adversity or challenge, how do you think these students would react in situations when they struggle? Is it reasonable to expect them to persevere or to be resilient in the face of challenge even though they have not experienced much success, do not feel confident in their abilities, and probably lack the knowledge of strategies to improve? Probably not.
>
> To overcome these challenges and failure experiences, many of your students need help – specifically they need guidance in how to think, interpret, and respond to these evaluation situations. So let's talk about some of the things you can do to provide this type of support."

This discussion tends to elicit a strong personal reaction from teachers because they all can identify students who struggle in school and who exhibit these maladaptive patterns of thinking and reaction. They also come to realize that because students are under a constant barrage of daily or weekly performance feedback, many students are continuously experiencing stress, anxiety, and frustration due to their persistent struggles.

It is my hope that after reading this chapter you will be better equipped to guide your students through this reflection process. That is, to get them to reflect on their grades and performance in school in a more adaptive and positive way, regardless of whether they achieve at a high or low level.

Core Concept 7.1

Many students will often experience that moment of receiving a graded assignment, exam, or project as an *intense, emotional event*.

● ● ● ● ●

What's in a Grade Anyway?

Our society places much emphasis on the importance of high achievement, competition, and striving to be the best. Across K-12 schools in our country, student accomplishments are routinely and publicly acknowledged and recognized. Whether this includes Honor Roll ceremonies, awards for High Achiever of the Month, or 1st, 2nd, and 3rd place ribbons given out at art shows or science fairs, our students are often conditioned to think about success in terms of how smart they are and how they measure up to others.

I can recall one situation when my son, who was in elementary school at the time, came home from school to tell me some exciting news. Apparently, his teacher informed the entire class that there was a student in the class who had earned one of the highest numerical test averages in math (within the top three of students) across the entire grade. He was excited to tell me this story because, as you might have guessed, he happened to be the student. After enthusiastically telling me (in precise detail of course) the words that his teacher conveyed to the class, he looked at me and grinned, "I am pretty smart I guess ... do you think I am smarter than most people?"

To be honest, I had mixed feelings about the situation. On one hand, I was very happy that he performed well and that he was so excited. However, I didn't want him to develop the habit of thinking about success in terms of his intelligence. I preferred that he think about his performance in terms of his behaviors and skills that directly led him to be successful. So after he finished speaking, I smiled and then attempted to reframe the situation. I reminded him about all of his behaviors and strategies that led him to be successful, such as completing his homework every night, doing extra enrichment math activities, playing video games that helped him develop his math fluency and other skills, and asking his teacher questions when confused.

I have to admit, though, on some level I was thrilled when I first heard the story. I mean, who doesn't want their kid to think of themselves as smart and intelligent, right? But, as I emphasized in Chapter 2 and will again discuss in this chapter (see section on attributions), when students get into the habit of reflecting on their grades in terms of intelligence or other "fixed" factors, they become vulnerable to experiencing inner turmoil when they struggle on something.

That said, let me qualify a few things about grades and self-reflection. First, I am not claiming that a focus on outcomes and grades in school is inherently a bad thing. Having to face competition and performance pressure will help prepare students to function and cope adaptively as school becomes more complex and once they eventually enter the workforce. There is also research showing that setting reasonably high self-standards for success (i.e., getting high grades in school) will often have positive effects on students' motivation and overall achievement (Schunk, Meece, & Pintrich, 2014). Further, grades and other forms of outcome feedback are valuable and needed to promote SRL. As I discussed in Chapters 5 (feedback) and 6 (self-monitoring), performance feedback and data enable individuals to address the question of, "How well did I do?" (self-evaluation).

In my opinion, the primary issue with such an intense focus on grades and outcomes is that most students *are rarely provided with structured opportunities and supportive contexts within which to process and interpret the meaning and relevance of their grades*. In this chapter, I lay the conceptual foundation for creating such opportunities and contexts. In short, this foundation is represented by three core reflection phase questions:

- How well did I do? (self-evaluation)
- Why did I perform that way? (attributions)
- What do I need to do to improve? (adaptive inferences)

Self-Evaluation ... Beginning the Self-Reflection Process

When students receive a grade or other types of feedback about an assignment, they will naturally think about *how well* they performed. From an SRL perspective, this process of making a judgment about performance is called *self-evaluation*. To self-evaluate, students need two pieces of information: an indicator of current performance (e.g., test grade) and a benchmark or standard (e.g., prior grades, norms, goals). Although students are flooded with information about grades and other performance feedback, they rarely receive guidance or assistance in *selecting the standard* against which to interpret those grades.

There are different types of standards that students can use to evaluate performance: *norms* ("how did I perform relative to my classmates?"), *externally-imposed standards* ("did my grade match with what my parents and teachers expect?"), *prior grades* ("was this grade higher or lower than my previous grades?"), or *personal goals* ("did I reach my goal?"). Take a minute to think about whether the specific standard that students use really makes a difference in their self-reflection skills. What do you think? In the following section, I illustrate how evaluative standards can have a direct influence on students' perceptions about success for failure and their subsequent reactions.

Success is in the Eye of the Beholder – The Case of Tanya

Suppose Tanya received scores of 70%, 63%, and 67%, respectively, on her last three science tests. Given her struggles in science and other subjects, Tanya's parents recently hired a tutor help her improve her learning and overall achievement. On a subsequent science exam, Tanya received a score of 77%. Before reading any further, please complete Reflect and Connect exercise 7.1.

Reflect and Connect – 7.1 The Self-Evaluation Process

Based on the information presented about Tanya in her science class:

- How do you think she will interpret her exam score of 77%? Will she conclude that she performed well or not so well?

_____

_____

Please read the following four scenarios about Tanya's self-evaluative standards and her subsequent reactions to her recent test grade of 77%. Each scenario is unique in terms of the self-evaluative standards that Tanya used to evaluate her grade. After you read these four scenarios, please complete Reflect and Connect exercise 7.2.

Scenario 1. Ms. Martinez recently finished grading a science exam. After handing back the test to her students, Ms. Martinez reviewed a few key concepts with the class. She also informed them that the class test average was about an 85%. Tanya began to feel anxious because her test grade was 8 points below the class average (*failure interpretation*). Part of the reason for her anxiety and frustration was her realization that she did not measure up well to her peers (*normative standards*). From her viewpoint, this test grade was further confirmation that she was not very smart and probably never would be.

Scenario 2. Ms. Martinez recently finished grading a science exam. After handing back the test to her students, Ms. Martinez reviewed a few key concepts with the class. She did not mention anything about the classroom average. Rather, she prompted the class to take out their self-monitoring graph and plot the current test grade (see Figure 7.1). When looking at her graph, Tanya noticed that her current grade of 77% was higher than all of her previous exams (*prior performance standards*); in fact, the current grade was 14 points higher than her lowest grade (63%). Tanya became somewhat hopeful because she felt that she may actually be improving (*success interpretation*).

Scenario 3. Ms. Martinez recently finished grading a science exam. After handing back the test to her students, Ms. Martinez reviewed a few key concepts with the class. She then instructed her students to take out their self-monitoring graph and plot the current grade (see Figure 7.2). She reminded them to think about how they performed by looking at the goal that they had set for themselves prior to the test. Using this graph, Tanya recognized that she did not reach her goal of 82% (*goal standard*), but she was getting much closer.

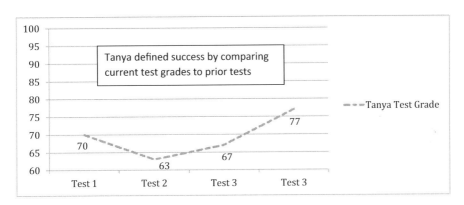

Figure 7.1 Tanya's self-evaluation judgments using prior test grades

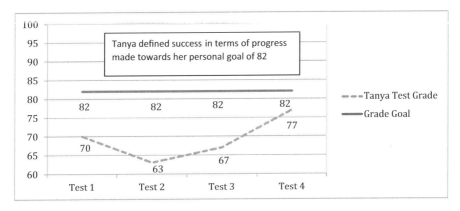

Figure 7.2 Tanya's self-evaluation judgments using a moderately challenging goal standard

108 Self-Reflection: Making Sense of Feedback

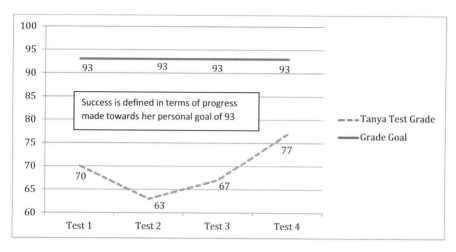

Figure 7.3 Tanya's self-evaluation judgments using a difficult goal standard

She noted, "Although I am not reaching my goal (a potential failure interpretation) I think I am improving" (*a success interpretation*). She felt more efficacious and began to exhibit higher motivation because she felt that she was actually making some progress.

Scenario 4. Ms. Martinez recently finished grading a science exam. After handing back the test to her students, Ms. Martinez reviewed a few key concepts with the class. She then instructed her students to plot their grades on the self-monitoring graph (see Figure 7.3). Similar to Scenario 3, Ms. Martinez reminded the class to compare their grade to their goal in order to assess how well that they did. After plotting her score of 77% on the graph and comparing it to her goal of 93% (*goal standard*), Tanya was extremely disappointed because she was still far away from her goal (*a failure interpretation*). From her perspective, this grade was just further confirmation that she could not do well in the class and that she really had no idea about what to do.

Reflect and Connect – 7.2 Reflecting on Tanya's Interpretations

- What are your thoughts about the differences in how Tanya interpreted her test score of 77% across the four scenarios?

_____
_____

- What is the primary take-away theme or conclusion you can make regarding her interpretations?

_____
_____

The Role of Self-Evaluation Standards

It is important to recognize that all self-evaluative standards (i.e., norms, prior performance, etc.) serve the same function or role in the regulatory process – simply put, they are *benchmarks* against which students make judgments about performance (Zimmerman, 2000). However, different standards lead to different interpretations of performance. Tanya believed that she had failed or performed poorly when using normative standards (scenario 1) or an excessively challenging goal standard (scenario 4); however, she felt successful when using prior test grades (scenario 2) or a more modest personal performance goal as the benchmark for success (scenario 3). What is interesting about Tanya's varying interpretations of performance was that from an objective point of view, *nothing had changed regarding her actual performance*. That is, she received a score of 77% on the most recent science test. The key variable was the type of benchmark or standard used to self-evaluate.

So what are the implications for teachers? First, it is important to recognize that the feedback messages and types of information you provide students can influence the type of self-evaluative standards they use to judge performance. Further, some standards appear to be more effective than others in promoting adaptive and strategic regulatory thinking and action. From my perspective, normative standards should be de-emphasized in K–12 school contexts. When teachers use normative evaluative practices, such as placing student grades on bulletin boards or verbally conveying class averages to the entire class, students will naturally gravitate towards focusing on their intelligence or the performance of others – things that they cannot change and control.

Although normative information can help students understand how they stack up to their peers, it can have many negative and unintended consequences. In some sense, normative standards work against an SRL mindset because they mask or obscure individual and personal growth. In looking back to Tanya scenario #1, her test score of 77% was 7–14 points *higher* than all other previous test scores. However, because Ms. Martinez prompted Tanya to focus on how she performed relative to her peers, Tanya did not notice this improvement. She was too preoccupied with the fact that she did not measure up to her classmates.

Core Concept 7.2

While *normative standards* enable students to understand how they compare to their peers, they lead students to evaluate themselves in terms of fixed factors, such as ability or intelligence.

Focusing on Self-Standards

From my perspective, teachers should encourage students to use evaluative standards that gets them to focus on their own personal skills, behaviors, and or grades. These standards include *prior performance, personal goals* or other benchmarks of mastery. As part of my Self-Regulation Empowerment Program (SREP) (Cleary, Velardi, & Schnaidman, 2017), SREP coaches are taught to help students interpret their grades on tests or other activities relative to prior performance as well as personal goals. As part of a graphing procedure that involves plotting test grades and personal goals (see Figure 7.4), students are naturally guided to address similar yet distinct self-evaluative questions: (a) "Is my performance improving over time? (prior performance as the standard), and (b) "Am I reaching my goal?" (personal goal as the standard).

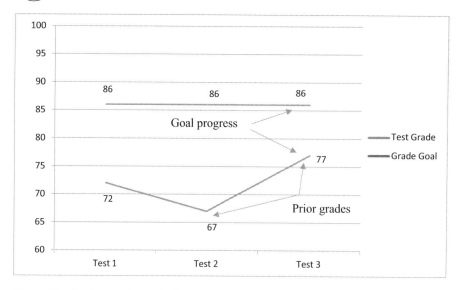

Figure 7.4 Using goals and prior grades as self-evaluative standards

Both of these standards are adaptive in that they direct students' attention to the "self." When used together they have the additional benefit of helping students develop a more nuanced interpretation and understanding of their outcomes. In looking back to Tanya scenario #3, she used prior performance and an outcome goal as self-evaluative standards. Because she was able to identify a positive trend in performance (prior performance standard) she viewed herself as being successful even though she had not yet reached her goal.

I would like to point out, however, that getting students to use self-standards will not automatically lead them to experience greater success. If students' grades are low and not improving over time, then it is an appropriate and valid reaction for them to conclude that they are not performing well. Along the same lines, it is very possible that students can establish a personal goal but may not ever be able to reach that goal. Scenario #4 with Tanya illustrates this point. Because her outcome goal of 93% was overly ambitious and difficult to obtain, Tanya was setting herself up to experience failure. Although her attempt to become more goal-directed should be encouraged in the future, when goals are not realistic and attainable, they can actually inhibit adaptive reflective thinking.

Core Concept 7.3

Getting students to use realistic *personal standards* (prior performance, personal goals) will help them to self-evaluate in a more personal and self-directed way.

Attributions ... Searching for the Reasons Why

Self-evaluation is the key first step in the self-reflection process. However, self-reflection involves more than simply answering "Did I succeed or not?" To become more successful over time, students need to ask additional questions such as, "Why did I perform this way?" and "How can I improve?"

Attribution theories posit that humans have a natural tendency to want to understand and master their worlds, and naturally search for reasons why they are successful or not – a regulatory process known as *causal attributions* (Weiner, 2010). This theoretical framework posits that people are most likely to search for explanations of performance in certain situations: when performance is poor, when the performance level was unexpected, and/or when the activity is valued (Schunk et al., 2014). In the case of Johanna, because she wants to get into a top-tier college and possesses exceedingly high standards for success, she places enormous value on performing well in all of her courses (see Tales of the Student – 7.3). Thus, when Johanna receives a sub-par grade on a test or assignment, she tends to check over the assignment to see if her teacher made a scoring error. She will also go back to her notes and study guide materials to figure out why she might have messed up some questions. In contrast, Tanya's approach to reflection is quite distinct. Given that Tanya is much younger than Johanna, she probably does not possess the same level of reflective skill. However, it is also relevant to point out that because Tanya expects to perform poorly and does not recognize the importance of doing well in school, she rarely ever wants to engage in self-reflection and analysis. Her reflections are fleeting and superficial and tend to focus on factors that can she cannot change or control (e.g., teacher difficulty, innate ability).

Tales of the Student – 7.3 Johanna

Johanna is currently enrolled in an Advanced Placement physics course. Unfortunately, she has not performed up to her self-imposed standards of getting A's on all assignments and tests. For example, over the past two weeks she received a B on a very comprehensive lab report and a B on an equally difficult unit exam. Although these grades were close to the class average, Johanna was frustrated because, "the grade of B does not measure up." Adding to her feelings of frustration and embarrassment was her teacher's (Mr. Filipo's) lighthearted comment while handing back the exam, "Wow … what is happening to one of my best students?" Johanna did not like that comment because she already puts enough pressure on herself and does not need other people to do the same. Of particular concern is that when Johanna receives a poor grade in this class, she blames her teachers for these difficulties and also begins to doubt her own abilities. Johanna is very anxious a lot of the time and just wants to make sure that this class does not ruin her overall GPA.

Reflect and Connect – 7.3 Revisiting Reader Reflection 7.1

I would like you to refer back to Reader Reflection activity 7.1.

- What types of attributions did you make following your struggle experience?

  _____

  _____

- How did these types of thoughts influence how you felt and how you responded?

  _____

  _____

Self-Reflection: Making Sense of Feedback

> **Attribution #1.** "It is obvious that I am no good at math. I was always bad at math and I will probably always not be good at it" (internal, stable, uncontrollable).
>
> **Attribution #2.** "My teacher goes too quickly in class. She is not a very good teacher" (external, stable, uncontrollable).

Figure 7.5 Tanya's attributions following a poor math test grade

● ● ● ● ●

Are Certain Attributions Better Than Others?

Before reading this section, please answer the two questions posed in Reflect and Connect exercise 7.3. The specific reasons or attributions you identified in this reflection exercise can be categorized across three broad dimensions: locus of origin, stability, and controllability (Weiner, 2010; Schunk et al., 2014). The *locus* dimension pertains to whether the cause comes from within (internal) or outside a person (external). The *stability* dimension involves whether the perceived cause is likely to stay the same or if it will likely change across situations and time. The final dimension, *controllability*, pertains to the extent to which individuals can influence, change, or modify the causes. I introduce these three dimensions because they influence how students think, feel, and react to a particular performance.

To illustrate the meaning of these dimensions, I refer back to Tanya (see Tales of the Student – 7.1). In this situation, Tanya made two distinct attributions regarding her grade of 77% (see Figure 7.5).

Attribution #1 (ability or competency) includes the following dimensions: internal, stable, and uncontrollable. It is *internal* because ability or skills operate within a person. Because most people tend to view ability as a relatively fixed construct (note: ability can be viewed as unstable if one adopts an incremental view of intelligence or a growth mindset – see Chapter 2), her attribution would also be considered *stable*. Finally, this attribution would be considered *uncontrollable* because Tanya clearly does not believe that she can modify or change how smart she is.

Attribution #2 (teacher difficulty) exhibits the same *stable* and *uncontrollable* characteristics (i.e., teacher difficulty is not easily changed; Tanya is not very likely to influence it). However, the two attributions can be differentiated along the *locus of origin* dimension. Whereas ability clearly has an internal locus (ability resides within the person), teacher difficulty reflects an external locus (it exists outside of the person). Why does this matter? Is it relevant that some attributions are uncontrollable vs controllable or internal vs. external?

Actually, it matters quite a bit. The type of attributions that students make about test grades and other performance outcomes in school has a direct impact on how they feel about themselves and school, their expectations for success, and their desire or motivation to keep trying hard even when struggling (Graham & Taylor, 2016; Schunk et al., 2014). In the following section, I use the Tanya scenarios to illustrate this point in greater detail.

The Dangers of Uncontrollable, Stable Attributions

The ability and teacher difficulty attributions that Tanya expressed regarding her test grade of 77% are *stable* and *uncontrollable*. Thus, regardless of whether the *locus* or *source* of the cause was internal (within Tanya) or external (outside of Tanya), Tanya will likely exhibit negative self-reactions because the perceived causes are not easily

Attribution	Likely thoughts and emotions	Potential behavioral reactions
Teacher question: What is the main reason why you failed your last test? **Student response**: The teacher is not very good and I just can't do math.	Low success expectations Helplessness Embarrassment Poor self-esteem	Superficial levels of effort Minimal persistence Withdrawal Oppositional behavior

Figure 7.6 Depiction of the link between uncontrollable attributions and student reactions

changed (stable) and that she has minimal influence over them (uncontrollability). I highlight the connection between uncontrollable, stable attributions following failure as well as the thoughts, emotions, and behaviors that typically follow (see Figure 7.6).

I would like to emphasize, however, that the *locus of origin* (whether the cause originated within or outside the person) dimension is not irrelevant. Let's consider Tanya's two attributions. The ability-focused attribution originates within her (internal), whereas teacher difficulty occurs outside of her (external). Although this distinction seems subtle, it can have quite a substantial effect on how Tanya experiences and reacts to failure.

Suppose Tanya placed primary weight on her poor ability as the primary cause of her poor grades. Thus, in addition to thinking that her struggles will likely occur in the future (high stability) and that she cannot effect change on her ability (low controllability), she now must also deal with the fact that *she is the source of the problem* (internal). That is, "**the cause of my failure is me, not them**." Students exhibiting this type of attribution pattern will tend to have negative self-perceptions and will say things like, "I am dumb" or "I am a bad student."

Conversely, suppose Tanya considered teacher difficulty as the primary cause of her struggles. By blaming others (i.e., "**the cause of my failure is them, not me**") Tanya gives herself a temporary reprieve. That is, there is a short-term mental health benefit from blaming others (i.e., preserved self-esteem and/or self-efficacy). Please note, however, that I am not recommending that students should place blame on teachers, parents, or peers for their struggles. Obviously, that is not good practice. My primary point here is to simply illustrate that different dimensions of attributions can have varying effects on the things that students pay attention to and how they subsequently feel and react to a performance situation.

Core Concept 7.4

Similar to self-evaluation, the process of *making causal attributions* is subjective and can directly influence how students subsequently think, feel, and react.

Shifting to Controllable Attributions

One of the most effective ways to empower and motivate your students is to help them recognize that they possess the capability and skills to overcome challenges and obstacles. One pathway to accomplish this is to teach your students to make *internal, unstable,* and *controllable* attributions. That is, you want students to think about things that reside within them, are malleable in nature, and can be directly influenced by them. The most useful attributions involve *effort* and *strategy use.* I will first consider effort attributions before turning to the "gold standard" of making strategic attributions.

Suppose you recently graded and handed back a test/assignment/paper to your students and asked them, *"What is the main reason why you got this grade?"* (an attribution question). What do you think your students who struggled on this assignment would say? Although there are numerous possibilities, some students will say things like, "I did not study" or "I did not really try very hard." These statements are often true in that they may not have put forth the necessary effort to perform well. Thus, getting students to openly admit that their poor grades were due to poor effort may nudge them to try harder.

Effort attributions, however, do not always lead to a desirable reaction because they are often vague and non-specific. Of greater concern is that they provide minimal guidance to students regarding *what* or *how* to change. That is, effort attributions only convey to students that they need to do more of "something," but what is that something? Another issue is that students will sometimes tell others that they did not try hard, even though they actually put forth much effort. Most students do not want others to perceive them as "dumb" or "stupid." Thus, if Tanya or Johanna told their classmates or teachers that they simply did not study or try very hard (even though they really did), they will likely feel less pressure or anxiety about how their friends or teachers judge their abilities. That is, from Tanya's or Johanna's perspective, "If I say I do not care and that I did not try very hard, then people probably won't think that I am incompetent."

Along a similar vein, consider the unintended side effects of Ms. Martinez encouraging students to make effort attributions following a test. Suppose after Tanya received the grade of 77% on the test, Ms. Martinez stated in a very well-intentioned and supportive way, *"You just need to try harder. If you put in more effort I know you can do it!"* Although this comment is seemingly encouraging and supportive, Tanya may not perceive it that way. In fact, what types of conclusions might Tanya make following this comment if Tanya believed that she was trying as hard as she possibly could? Right … that she probably lacks the capacity to perform well on the activity.

From my perspective, the most adaptive and effective type of attribution that students can make following performance involves the task processes, strategies, or specific behaviors that are linked to successful performance on that task. Thus, if Tanya believes that the primary reason for her poor performance was due to her insufficient use of strategies (e.g., poor time management skills when studying, not correctly representing the word problems as a picture), her subsequent reflective thoughts and feelings would likely center on her own *behavior,* rather than her poor intelligence or the inadequacy of her teacher (see Figure 7.7). Consistent with the research literature, when students attribute poor performance to *effort using strategies,* they will likely exhibit a more positive sense of self and can develop ideas about specific things they need to improve (Cleary, Zimmerman, & Keating, 2006; Graham & Taylor, 2016; Schunk et al., 2014). That is, "**the cause is NOT me as a person … the cause is NOT others … the cause is the strategies and skills I used (or did not use) when completing the activity.**"

You might be wondering whether strategic attributions are similar to the concept of a growth mindset discussed in Chapter 2. They do overlap to some degree. For students who make strategic attributions or exhibit a growth mindset, they do not view failure or struggling in school as a pre-determined outcome resulting from innate incompetency or inability; rather, they perceive failure as an opportunity to grow through effort and use of task-focused or SRL-focused strategies. Making strategic attributions,

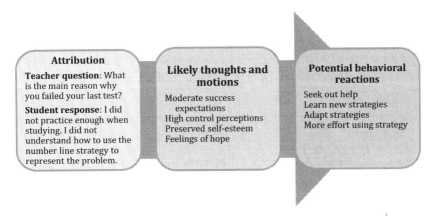

Figure 7.7 Depiction of link between strategic attributions and student reactions

adopting a growth mindset, and experiencing high self-efficacy are all things that give students a sense of "hope" which subsequently guides them to think about ways to adapt and improve their lives.

Core Concept 7.5

Another useful way to get students to THINK IN THE LANGUAGE OF STRATEGIES is by prompting them to attribute success or failure to their own behaviors and strategy use.

Encouraging Adaptive Reflection in Classrooms

As I state repeatedly throughout this book, it is essential that teachers get students to THINK IN THE LANGUAGE OF STRATEGIES during all aspects of the learning process. Thus, whenever I use this phrase, I am referring to the importance of having students think about strategies *before* they start a learning activity, *during* the learning activity, and *after* completing the activity. While the previous chapters emphasized strategic thinking when setting goals, developing task plans, and self-monitoring, the current chapter focuses on strategic thinking during self-reflection.

Classroom-Based Reflection Activities

In Figure 7.8, I summarize different tactics that teachers can use to get their students to reflect in more strategic ways about performance outcomes. In reviewing this figure, you will probably notice that I have already discussed the majority of these recommendations in previous chapters. However, the one instructional tactic that I still need to address involves how teachers can engage students in structured reflection activities during classroom activities.

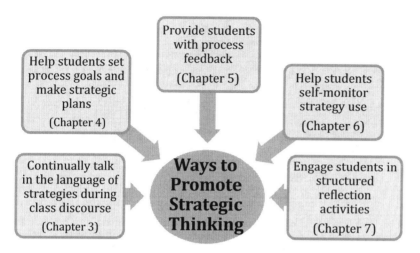

Figure 7.8 Tactics to enhance strategic self-reflection in students

It is my belief that most students do not receive the necessary guidance and supports to adaptively reflect on their grades and performance in school. A typical process for providing feedback might entail teachers handing back graded papers or projects and then asking students to review their mistakes. Some teachers may also engage their class in a discussion about common mistakes, important themes, or other relevant ideas about the assignment or project. Others may even request students to redo or resubmit some of the work. While all of these reflection practices can be helpful, students will often need more direct coaching and prompting to adequately process and use the performance feedback to improve.

Getting students to reflect adaptively about their grades is not a trivial matter. From my perspective, all teachers have the potential to engage students in a positive and collaborative reflective exchange. As part of this discourse, students can be encouraged to ask questions and to clarify misconceptions about their knowledge and understanding of concepts. In recent years, researchers have emphasized the importance of *feedback dialogues* – an ongoing, reciprocal exchange between the feedback provider (teacher) and the recipient (student; Nicol & Macfarlane-Dick, 2006). The basic idea of a feedback dialogue is to create a climate and structure that encourages and enables students to process and reflect on the meaning and purpose of performance information or feedback. This experience should culminate in students being more likely to *use that feedback* to direct their own behaviors in the future.

You might be reading this section and agree with the basic premise that getting students to process and reflect on feedback is important and that such reflection activities can lead to positive student outcomes. But you may also be wondering, "*How do I this?,*" and from a more pragmatic viewpoint, "*Do I have the time to engage students in feedback dialogues during class?*" Clearly, there are many barriers to engaging students in deep, meaningful reflection activities. You might have limited experience in this realm and may not have the time during class to devote to these activities. In addition, it is not possible to have in-depth, lengthy dialogues with all of your students. Despite these challenges, there are several things that most teachers CAN do to promote healthy forms of self-reflection in their classrooms.

Devote at least 5–10 minutes for reflection. For any assignment, project or test that you believe is of "high value," allot at least 5–10 minutes to get students to reflect on and evaluate their grades or other feedback (see Chapters 8 and 9). Without having a dedicated or structured time for students to think about their grades, the likelihood that they will do so on their own and in a productive manner is fairly low.

Consider using group reflection activities. Having one-on-one reflective conversations with students is an ideal context from which you can provide assistance to individual students. However, this is not realistic and may not even be needed in all circumstances, teachers should consider using group self-reflection activities. As part of SREP, students receive extensive support and coaching for self-reflection training (Cleary et al., 2017). For example, after students receive a test grade back from their teacher, the SREP coach asks students to complete a reflection worksheet. On this worksheet, students are asked to record their exam grades, their perceptions of success or failure (*self-evaluation*), the reasons why they might have earned that grade (*attributions*) and potential solutions to areas of struggle (*adaptive inferences*). Students are then encouraged to share their reactions with their classmates in small groups of 5–6 students. The SREP coaches facilitate this conversation and gradually guide the groups to focus on the most effective strategies that can lead to enhanced performance on future tests.

In Chapters 8–9, I provide an extended discussion of how the SREP reflection process can be applied to classroom activities. In short, teachers can ask their students to individually answer a few questions about their performance that mirror several self-reflection processes (i.e., self-evaluation, causal attributions, adaptive inferences). Students can then break up into small groups to process and share their thinking with each other, while their teacher provides support and guidance.

Use peers to facilitate the reflection process. To alleviate some of the burden that teachers experience in terms of class size management and constrained instructional time, teachers can use students who exhibit "adaptive reflection" skills to serve as co-facilitators in the reflection process. Researchers have begun to show that peers can be particularly effective in serving as co-participants in a feedback dialogue (Brookhart, 2008). In the case of Tanya, Ms. Martinez typically provides many written comments on assignments and projects. Because most of the class does not typically read or reflect on these comments, Ms. Martinez decided to organize students in small "feedback dialogue" peer groups to facilitate processing of this feedback. In forming the groups, Ms. Martinez made sure to include at least one student who displays adaptive reflection skills. Ms. Martinez then prompted each student within the groups to do two things: (a) review their own work, and (b) identify one comment made by others that was interesting, useful, or helpful. Each person then shares these perceptions with the group, while Ms. Martinez walks around the room to clear up misconceptions and to offer relevant insights.

Concluding Thoughts

The topic of self-reflection represents the culminating concept in the cyclical, SRL feedback process. In short, it is important to get students to engage in self-reflection after they have: (1) used strategies to learn or perform some activity, (2) self-monitored their thoughts, behaviors, or performance, and/or (3) received feedback from teachers or others about their skills or grades. As part of an effective reflection activity, it is important to get students to pause and think about three key questions:

- How well did I do in relation to my prior grades or personal goals?
- What are the key strategies or skills that led me to receiving this grade?
- How do I need to adapt or change these strategies to improve in the future?

The first two sections of this book helped to develop the conceptual foundation of SRL while also illustrating how several SRL principles (e.g., goals, strategies, self-monitoring, self-reflection) can be applied to classroom contexts. In the final section, *Bringing it All Together* (Chapters 8–9), I illustrate how teachers can integrate these SRL principles in a simple and straightforward, yet coherent and comprehensive way. Using two common situations experienced by most teachers (i.e., test preparation and test review classroom activities, and classroom-based projects), the final section of the book provides a roadmap for SRL-immersed instructional activities.

● ● ● ● ●

References

Brookhart, S. M. (2008). *How to give effective feedback to your students*. Alexandria, VA: Association for Supervision and Curriculum Development.

Cleary, T. J., Velardi, B., & Schnaidman, B. (2017). Effects of the Self-Regulated Empowerment Program (SREP) on middle school students' strategic skills, self-efficacy, and mathematics achievement. *Journal of School Psychology, 64*, 28–42.

Cleary, T. J., Zimmerman, B. J., & Keating, T. (2006). Training physical education students to self-regulate during basketball free throw practice. *Research Quarterly for Exercise and Sport, 77*(2), 251–262.

Graham, S., & Taylor, A. Z. (2016). Attribution theory and motivation in school. In K. R. Wentzel & D. B. Miele (Eds.), *Handbook of motivation at school* (pp. 11–33). New York: Routledge.

Nicol, D. J., & Macfarlane-Dick, D. (2006). Formative assessment and self-regulated learning: A model and seven principles of good feedback practice. *Studies in Higher Education, 31*(2), 199–218. doi:10.1080/03075070600572090.

Schunk, D. H., Meece, J. L., & Pintrich, P. R. (2014). *Motivation in education: Theory, research, and applications* (4th ed.). Upper Saddle River, NJ: Pearson Education.

Weiner, B. (2010). The development of an attribution-based theory of motivation: A history of ideas. *Educational Psychologist, 45*(1), 28–36. doi:10.1080/00461520903433596.

Zimmerman, B. J. (2000). Attaining self-regulation: A social-cognitive perspective. In M. Boekaerts, P. Pintrich, & M. Zeidner (Eds.), *Self-regulation: Theory, research, and applications* (pp. 13–39). Orlando, FL: Academic Press.

Section III

Bringing It All Together

8

Teaching SRL Skills: Classroom Testing Activities

I believed in studying just because I knew education was a privilege. It was the discipline of study, to get into the habit of doing something that you don't want to do.
—Wynton Marsalis

 Chapter Snapshot

In this chapter, I illustrate how teachers can embed SRL principles into classroom-based test preparation and test review activities. After summarizing common challenges that students and teachers encounter in the days and weeks leading up to and following classroom tests, I present a case study to illustrate SRL implementation practices. Specifically, I describe the experiences of Ms. Walsh, a 9th grade social studies teacher as she attempts to integrate SRL principles in her classroom. I also present detailed conversations between Ms. Walsh and Angie, a student teacher, to convey Ms. Walsh's thought process and underlying reasoning for using specific SRL applications and innovations.

Reader Reflection – 8.1 Test-Taking In Your Class

Try to recall the last major test or quiz that you administered in your class. As you think about this test/quiz, please answer the following questions:

- What types of guidance or support did you provide students in the weeks or days leading up to the test/quiz? What did you say or do to help them prepare more effectively?

  _____
  _____

- After grading the test/quiz and giving it back to students, did you have them reflect on the test/quiz or did you get them to think about or do anything it? If so, what did you ask them to do?

  _____
  _____

Introduction

In today's schools, students are confronted with a variety of testing situations. As part of national, state, and/or school-wide testing initiatives, school districts administer standardized tests to evaluate the growth of their students' achievement levels and academic skills. Some students also take tests to determine their eligibility for certain educational programs (e.g., Special Education, gifted programs) or as part of college preparation requirements (e.g., SAT, ACT). Although each of these standardized testing situations serves an important purpose, they represent a relatively small fraction of the testing experiences that students encounter in schools. In fact, if I asked a random group of middle school or high school students about the most common testing experience, I suspect most of them would talk about the tests they take in their content-area courses rather than the more global standardized tests.

As I begin this chapter, a reasonable question to ask is why would I devote an entire chapter to SRL and classroom-based testing activities? One of the reasons is that classroom-based tests represent a universal experience for students in most classroom and school contexts. Thus, whether thinking about Tanya, Michael, Peter, or Johanna, most students have experienced preparing for, taking, and receiving feedback about classroom tests or quizzes (see Tales of the Teacher – 8.1). Another reason is that tests often represent the primary way for teachers to evaluate student learning and thus are heavily weighted when calculating students' report card grades. For this latter reason, the experience of taking tests and receiving feedback about one's performance tends to represent a high-stakes, emotional event for students, particularly for those like Tanya who struggle in school. In this chapter, I provide a basic framework illustrating how teachers can help students approach and react to the classroom testing experience in a more empowered and adaptive way.

Tales of the Teacher – 8.1 Typical Approaches to Testing

Ms. Walsh is a 9th grade social studies teacher who gives a test to her students approximately every three to four weeks. At the start of each unit, Ms. Walsh likes to tell her students about the anticipated date for the next exam so that they can appropriately plan and think ahead. Despite doing this, many of her students do not begin preparing for the tests in advance. In fact, most students will not think about the test at all until she hands out the review packet a couple of days before the exam.

As part of the review packet, Ms. Walsh lists the most essential topics and terms and provides examples of important questions that students may want to consider as they study. After distributing the study guide, she typically reviews it with students and gives them an opportunity to ask questions at that time or at any point prior to the exam.

Ms. Walsh is a strong believer in providing immediate feedback to students, so she typically returns student exams within a day or two. When reviewing the exams, Ms. Walsh highlights the key questions that most students got wrong on the exam. She also talks with them about the class test average so that they can get a better sense of their performance. In most instances, Ms. Walsh also gives students an opportunity to attend after-school feedback sessions to obtain additional assistance, if needed. Although most students do not take her up on her offer, the students who often attend these sessions are, ironically, the solid performers in class.

Classroom-Based Tests: Student Challenges

In a simplistic sense, classroom-based testing is a process whereby students are exposed to course content during class lectures and activities, are asked to complete homework and other assignments to support classroom learning, and then direct their own behaviors to study for the exam (hopefully!). Students then take the test and are provided feedback from their teacher. Although this process sounds fairly straightforward and simple, it is fraught with many potential pitfalls and obstacles for students.

To adequately learn and recall information, students need to have sufficient knowledge and competence in using *study skills*; an umbrella term that overlaps conceptually with strategy terms, such as *task-focused* and *self-regulation strategies*, that I previously discussed (Richardson, Robnolt, & Rhodes, 2010; see also Chapter 3). Thus, study skills include methods that enhance time management, learning and retention of information, organization of materials, seeking support from others, and note-taking (Hattie & Donoghue, 2016; Karabenick & Berger, 2013; Richardson et al., 2010; Weinstein & Acee, 2013). Given the importance of these strategies, an essential instructional question for teachers to consider is, *"When, where, and how can I help students learn about these strategic skills?"*

Another challenge for students is developing an understanding of the circumstances and/or situations when they need to adapt or change their typical studying methods. As I discussed in Chapter 1, students need to adapt when the *rules of the game* change, such as when taking a difficult mathematics class or when transitioning from elementary school to middle school and then on to high school. Specifically, during the secondary school years, students are instructed by a team of teachers who typically differ in the frequency with which they administer classroom tests, the types of test questions that are emphasized (e.g., multiple choice, matching, short answer, essays), or perhaps even the standards that they use to evaluate student performance. If you think back to the difficulties that Johanna experienced in her physics class (see Tales of the Student – 3.2), one reason for her struggles was her rigid adherence to a study approach that, although previously successful, was no longer working in some classes. Thus, as teachers develop and construct tests, it is important for them to think about, *"Is there any way I can increase student awareness about how to match their study approach to the specific aspects of the test?"*

Test preparation involves much more than reviewing information that was presented during classroom instruction. As students progress through the K-12 years and encounter more rigorous coursework, a large percentage of learning occurs outside of school. Because students are faced with this task of assuming greater personal responsibility to direct and navigate their own learning, another relevant question for teachers is, *"Are there things that I can do to help students more effectively manage their studying and test preparation outside the classroom?"*

Finally, student motivation is often a problem in school contexts. As I discussed in Chapter 2, students may disengage or not put forth the necessary effort to prepare due to:

- a lack of or inadequate goals
- low self-efficacy perceptions
- lack of awareness regarding the value or importance of the learning activity
- a fixed mindset.

Thus, a final thing that teachers should be cognizant of as they develop test preparation activities is, *"How can I influence student perceptions and beliefs so that they try harder and persist when studying at home?"*

Reflect and Connect – 8.1 Thinking About Student Thinking

Refer back to Reader Reflection activity 8.1. Specifically, focus on the second question about self-reflection. When you return tests to your students, to what extent do you truly know:

- how well your students prepared for the test?
- the types of things they thought about and felt when looking at their test grade?
- their understanding of the things that are necessary to perform well on the next test?

Classroom-Based Tests: Teacher Challenges

Before reading this section, I encourage you to complete Reflect and Connect exercise 8.1. In addition to helping students overcome their personal challenges in preparing for tests, teachers face their own set of challenges. Although teachers have control over some aspects of the testing process, such as developing meaningful and appropriate tests and providing timely performance feedback, they are left in the dark regarding the things their students do, think about, and feel during test preparation activities at home. As soon as the bell rings at the end of the school day, teachers can only wonder, "Are my students focused on the right material when studying?", "Are students practicing and using strategies in an effective way?" or "Are students spending enough time studying and preparing?" This lack of awareness is a problem because it restricts your capacity as a teacher to provide useful feedback to students about how to change or adapt their study strategies. Thus, a specific area of challenge for teachers involves, *"How can I become more knowledgeable about the process that students engage in when preparing for tests?"*

Another challenge for teachers involves balancing the amount of time needed for classroom testing process (e.g., helping students prepare for tests, developing and administering tests, reviewing tests with students) relative to instructional time. Obviously, teachers need to devote some class time to administering the test, but how much class time should they allocate to test preparation and test review activities? Given that many students struggle to adequately plan for and reflect on their classroom tests, another challenging question for teachers is, *"What is the most efficient and effective way for me to engage students in planning and self-reflection activities about their test performance?"*

Core Concept 8.1

Try to become aware of and reflect on the challenges that you and your students encounter in the days and weeks leading up to a classroom test.

SRL Lesson Plan – Getting Students Prepped Before the Test

Ms. Walsh developed a 60–65 minute instructional approach for infusing SRL principles in test preparation and test review activities conducted within her classroom (see Tales of the Teacher – 8.2). This block of instructional time was spread out across several class sessions over a three-week period.

Tales of the Teacher – 8.2 Embarking on a New Instructional Path

Ms. Walsh recently began educating herself about student self-regulated learning (SRL) and motivation. She recently attended a workshop and read a couple of books on SRL that were recommended by her colleagues. Although she learned many things, there were three key ideas that resonated most strongly with her:

- Test preparation should be an **on-going process** inside and out of school; it is not something that should be briefly discussed a day or two before an exam.
- Getting students to **think ahead** and to **reflect** on their learning can be just as important as the time that students spend studying course material.
- It is critical to get students to **THINK IN THE LANGUAGE OF STRATEGIES** as they prepare for and reflect on tests.

These ideas nudged Ms. Walsh to begin thinking about her approach to testing activities in her classroom. But she needed help about what to do next. One of her colleagues who also attended the PD training developed a guide to help him think about important questions when attempting to infuse SRL into his lessons. This guide was fairly simple in that it contained five key questions. Ms. Walsh decided to tweak this guide so that it reflected important questions related to test preparation and test review in her classroom (see Figure 8.1). All of the guiding questions began with the phrase, "How can I help students to …" and then ended with a specific theme of SRL and/or motivation; task analysis, planning, feedback and self-monitoring, self-reflection, and motivation.

Test Preparation Plan

Monday, March 1 (10 minutes). Ms. Walsh began a new unit on historical world cultures (e.g., Byzantine Empire). She informed the class that the next course exam would occur in approximately three weeks (Tuesday, March 23). Rather than simply telling her students about the exam date and proceeding with the lesson, however, she wanted to get students to focus their attention on test preparation. She developed and handed out two forms: *Test Preparation* worksheet (see Figure 8.2) and *Study Plan* worksheet (see Figure 8.3). Although Ms. Walsh did not require her students to begin completing these worksheets on this day, she reviewed and explained the characteristics and purposes of each form. The *Test Preparation* worksheet was designed to help students organize several important pieces of information about the test:

- relevant materials (book chapters, handouts, etc.)
- key topics, themes, or concepts that may appear on the test
- topics that are personally challenging for students
- format and structure of prior tests and the upcoming test.

How can I help students to...

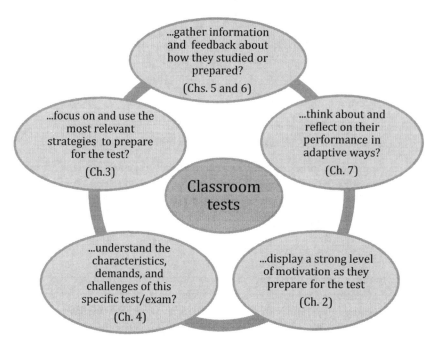

Figure 8.1 Instructional prompt to guide SRL test preparation and review activities

What assignments/quizzes/ other work that you completed in this unit will be on the next exam?	What are the major concepts/"big ideas"/key terms that you think will be on the next test?	What topics/ideas/concepts in this unit are challenging for you to learn?
• _____ • _____ • _____ • _____ • _____	• _____ • _____ • _____ • _____ • _____	• _____ • _____ • _____ • _____

What things prevent you from completing your work?	What WAS the format of the last test?	What WILL be the format of the next test?
☐ I often feel unmotivated to study ☐ I have trouble remembering facts ☐ I do not know how to ask for help ☐ I struggle to take good notes in class ☐ I forget my study materials at school ☐ I do not have enough time to study ☐ I get distracted by others ☐ I do not understand class lectures	☐ Multiple choice ☐ True/False ☐ Diagrams/models ☐ Short answer ☐ Essay ☐ Solving problems ☐ Other _____	☐ Multiple choice ☐ True/False ☐ Diagrams/modes ☐ Short answer ☐ Essay ☐ Solving problems ☐ Other _____

Figure 8.2 Example of a test preparation worksheet

Date of test _____ Date to begin studying: _____

Where will I study: _____

Most important thing for me to remember and focus on when studying: _____

TASK STRATEGIES	PLAN	TRIED	SRL STRATEGIES	PLAN	TRIED
Mnemonic device	☐	☐	Use strategies to manage time	☐	☐
Concept maps	☐	☐	Use motivation strategies	☐	☐
Self-quizzing	☐	☐	– positive self-talk	☐	☐
Identify question types	☐	☐	– rewards, tangibles	☐	☐
Create timelines of events	☐	☐	Organize my notes & materials	☐	☐
Summarize/re-write notes	☐	☐	Study in a comfortable place	☐	☐
Practice completing figures	☐	☐	Avoid distractions	☐	☐
Practice writing essays	☐	☐	Ask for help as needed	☐	☐
Other: _____	☐	☐	Look up info (textbooks, internet)	☐	☐
Other: _____	☐	☐	Other _____	☐	☐
Other: _____	☐	☐	Other _____	☐	☐

Are there any things that are preventing me from studying or doing my work?

☐ I often feel "unmotivated" to study   ☐ I forget my study materials in school
☐ I have trouble remembering facts   ☐ I do not have enough time to study
☐ I have trouble understanding how concepts work   ☐ I forget to study or do my homework
☐ I take very bad notes in class   ☐ I get distracted by others (phone, texts)

Figure 8.3 Example of Study Plan worksheet

In contrast, the *Study Plan* worksheet represented a guide to help students identify the different task-focused and SRL-focused strategies that students could use to prepare for the next exam. It also helps students track the challenges or barriers that they need to overcome during test preparation.

Friday, March 5 (7–8 minutes). Ms. Walsh gave her students approximately 5–7 minutes to begin recording relevant information about the upcoming test on the *Test Preparation* worksheet. Students were encouraged to ask questions and to collaborate with their classmates within their assigned work groups of 3–4 students.

Wednesday, March 10 (10 minutes). Ms. Walsh devoted the first 10 minutes of class to reviewing some strategies for organizing the information presented for that unit. She asked her students to take out the *Study Plan* worksheet from their binders and spoke with them about two strategies that she had previously discussed in class: *compare and contrast* tables and a *concept map*. As a brief reminder, she modeled how to use the concept map to integrate important facts introduced during the previous lesson.

Friday, March 12 (7–8 minutes). Towards the end of class, Ms. Walsh asked students to get into their assigned groups. The students worked collaboratively for approximately 7–8 minutes on the *Test Preparation* worksheet. Given the class was already about two weeks into the new unit, Ms. Walsh encouraged her students to identify any content or ideas that were challenging for them and, if they had time, to identify task-focused and SRL strategies on the *Study Plan* worksheet that could address those challenges.

128 Teaching SRL Skills: Classroom Testing Activities

Wednesday, March 14 (8–10 minutes). Given that self-quizzing is a very important learning strategy (Dunlosky et al., 2013), Ms. Walsh reminded her students to begin thinking about how to quiz themselves (or with the help of others) at home when studying. The students were knowledgeable about this technique given that it had been discussed during prior units. Ms. Walsh also gave students access to a bank of review questions and reminded them about using Quizlet as a way to self-assess their learning.

Friday, March 19 (10 minutes). The Friday before the exam, Ms. Walsh read through her typical study guide with students (i.e., key topics, questions, terms, etc.). She instructed them to get into their workgroups to make sure that they were aware of the specific content and principles that might appear on the exam. She also prompted the students to note whether they had all of the necessary materials to study. Ms. Walsh walked around the room to guide students and to answer any questions as they reviewed the *Test Preparation* and *Study Plan* worksheets.

Monday, March 22 (8–10 minutes). Ms. Walsh asked her students to take out the *Test Preparation* worksheet and to think about any challenges or barriers that were still giving them difficulty. Students were encouraged to ask any final questions.

Tuesday, March 23. As students came into the class to take the test, Ms. Walsh asked the students to turn in their *Test Preparation* worksheet. She then administered the test.

Reflect and Connect – 8.2 Test Preparation in Classrooms

- To what extent do you think the Test Preparation worksheet, or some variation of it, can be useful to you as part your classroom activities?

  _____

  _____

Conversations With Ms. Walsh – 8.1 Test Preparation Activities

Ms. Walsh frequently meets with Angie, one of her student teachers, to debrief about the learning activities and/or student behaviors during class. Following the March 22 class, Angie approached Ms. Walsh about the new test preparation activities that were used in class.

Angie: I know you told me about the different worksheets you developed for the class, but I never really asked you about them. Do you think they were really necessary?

Ms. Walsh: I actually think they are very important. As you know, some of our students really struggle on tests. Many of them have weak organizational skills and they seem to avoid things that are challenging. I also do not think that they are very strategic when preparing for tests. They just seem to do the same thing over and over without changing anything. Thus, I felt that I needed to do something differently ... something to change their thinking and approach to prepare for the tests. Using the Test Preparation worksheet was my attempt to increase their awareness about the test content and components, while the Study Plan worksheet got them to think about how they may want to approach studying.

Angie: You seemed to devote so much time and effort to the worksheets during class. Doesn't this take away too much time from instruction?

Ms. Walsh: It might take some time away, but take a look at my planner. I only spent about an hour or so of instructional time on test preparation over the past three weeks … which is not too bad. Also, because this unit was the first time that I tried to get students to pause and reflect on their approach to test preparation, I suspect we will become more efficient at doing these things. The funny thing is that it was not until I began reading and learning about SRL that I even realized that I had the skills or capacity to influence how students might approach test preparation and studying.

Angie: When I was walking around the room, I noticed that some of the students did not complete much of the Test Preparation worksheet.

Ms. Walsh: I know. That concerned me at first but I was not going to push the issue. This was the first time using the worksheet so I think a few students may resist it for now. They may not really understand its value and how it can help them. I do not think it makes sense to be overly controlling about it at this point. I am trying to open students' minds to possibilities about how they might want to change their behaviors when studying. Even if they do not complete the entire worksheet, I still think they can benefit from witnessing the enthusiasm and positive thinking exhibited by some of their classmates. Students can sometimes learn as much by observing as they can by doing it themselves.

Angie: I think I understand, but I am still not sure that students will benefit all that much. What would you say is the biggest thing you are trying to accomplish? And were all of these "add on" activities needed?

Ms. Walsh: Those are good questions. One of the purposes of having students complete those worksheets and engaging them in conversations about strategies is to elevate their consciousness and awareness about what to focus on when preparing for tests. I am very much committed to the concept of getting students to THINK IN THE LANGUAGE OF STRATEGIES on a more frequent basis. Thus, I want them to become more strategic in how they approach studying … to use different strategies and to tweak those strategies over time so that they can improve. When students go into high school and then hopefully to college, they need to be able to direct their own learning. In some sense, I view the things I am doing now as a way of planting seeds for them to become a self-regulated learner.

Angie: I think I get it. Initially, I thought that those worksheets were simply busy work. But I guess they are not really "extra" things to do.

Ms. Walsh: Exactly. All of the activities and worksheets we had them complete go hand-in-hand with the content of the class. They complement and inform each other.

Angie: Do you want me to look over the worksheets that they submitted? I think it would be interesting to delve into the things that they were thinking about.

Ms. Walsh: I was going to do that, but go ahead and take the first stab at it. I think reviewing these forms will give us a much better sense about how they think and approach test preparation. When we return the test in a few days, we can use this information as part of a reflection activity that I am planning to use with the class.

Teaching SRL Skills: Classroom Testing Activities

Core Concept 8.2

Reflecting on the phrase *THINKING IN THE LANGUAGE OF STRATEGIES* can serve as a useful prompt for you when developing lesson plans and when interacting with students.

Reflect and Connect – 8.3 Test Debriefing

Think back to the most recent test that you administered to your class.

- Did you follow a particular process when returning and/or reviewing the test with your students? Specifically, what did you do?

  _____

  _____

- Did you have a clear sense of the things that most of your students thought about and/ or felt after they received their test? How do you know?

  _____

  _____

SRL Lesson Plan – Reflecting on Test Performance

Before delving into Ms. Walsh's approach to reviewing tests with her class, I encourage you to complete Reflect and Connect exercise 8.3. In reflecting on her typical approach to reviewing tests with her class, Ms. Walsh felt the need to make some changes (see Tales of the Teacher – 8.3). She recognized that she rarely had students pause and think about what the test grade meant to them or, more importantly, why they may have performed that way. She also realized that most of her students who struggled on tests were not getting much feedback about their *approach* to test preparation nor did they receive information about *how they could adapt or change*. In addition, Ms. Walsh figured out that her practice of telling her students about the class test average may have been adversely affecting some of them, particularly those who struggled. Although Ms. Walsh's self-assessment revealed that she needed to improve some areas, she felt energized from her realization that making some tweaks to how she reviewed tests might make a big difference in how her students felt and reacted.

Tales of the Teacher – 8.3 Shifting to Self-Reflection

Traditionally, Ms. Walsh returned tests, quizzes, and other assignments to her students within two to three days. She is a staunch advocate of providing timely feedback to students, particularly regarding graded assignments. Her typical approach to debriefing or reviewing the tests with students involved highlighting three key themes that most students mastered (to reinforce some positive ideas) along with a few questions or concepts that were challenging for them. She feels that it is too difficult to provide individualized feedback to all of her students so she tends to talk about overall class patterns and themes. During this debriefing, Ms. Walsh also shared information about the class test average with students so they could more easily understand how well they performed. She reminded students that they could attend her after-school test review sessions to discuss concerns or to ask questions. Much to her chagrin, however, few students actually show up for these sessions.

Test Reflection Plan

On Thursday, March 25 (two days after students took the test), Ms. Walsh handed students a packet with three things: their graded tests, their *Test Preparation* worksheet, and a folder called, *My Reflection Folder*. In each folder was a copy of an *SRL graph* (Cleary & Platten, 2013; see Figure 8.4) and a *Self-Reflection* form (Cleary & Platten, 2013; see Figure 8.5). Ms. Walsh had previously introduced the graph and reflection form to students, but this was the first time she was going to use the form to guide student reflection.

Graphing Outcomes and Processes. When Ms. Walsh began the world history unit a few weeks ago, she introduced the *SRL graph* to students. At that time, she asked students to plot their last two test scores and to set a test grade goal – a grade that they wanted to achieve on their next test. During this goal-setting process, Ms. Walsh helped guide student thinking by telling them that an effective goal should be a little bit beyond their current achievement level but one that was not overly difficult or challenging.

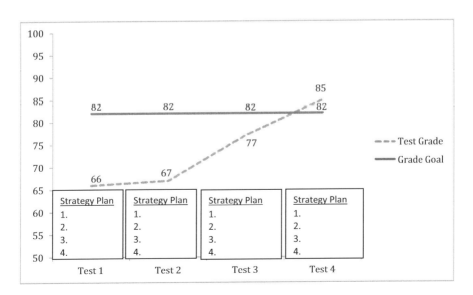

Figure 8.4 Self-Regulated Learning (SRL) graph

Teaching SRL Skills: Classroom Testing Activities

As part of the current test review session, Ms. Walsh prompted her students to take out their *SRL graph* and to plot the test grade. She then shifted student attention to their *Test Preparation* worksheet. She asked them to review this worksheet and then write down in the Strategy Plan box on the *SRL graph* the primary strategies they used to prepare for the test. Thus, the *SRL graph* included three key pieces of information: grade goals, actual test grades, and task-focused and/or SRL-focused strategies (see Figure 8.4). As I will discuss in the next section of this chapter, this graph served as the primary instructional tool from which Ms. Walsh guided classroom-based student reflection activities.

Promoting Individualized Reflection

To get the students started in the reflection process, Ms. Walsh addressed the class:

> "OK ... Now that everyone has finished with the graph, I want you to answer some questions. Using the Self-Reflection form, I want you to think about whether you believe you performed well or not [self-evaluation], how satisfied you are with the grade [satisfaction], why you think you performed this way [attribution], and some of the things that you believe you need to do to perform well on the next test [adaptive inference]. But let me give you a tip when answering each of these questions. For the first question, try to evaluate yourself using two different standards ... the goals that you had set for yourself and the grades you received on prior tests. Thus, did you reach your goal? Was this grade higher or lower than your prior test grade?" For the second question, just think about how satisfied you are with the grade and why you feel this way.
>
> For the third question, I am asking you to write down all of the things that you believe influenced how well you did on this test. That is, what are the primary reasons why you performed that way? There are no right or wrong answers, so be as open and honest as you can. If you don't know, that is OK ... simply write that you don't know.
>
> Finally, for the last question, think about and write down the things that you believe are most important for you to do to perform well on the next test. Is there anything that you would do the same? What would you need to do differently?"

Ms. Walsh then gave the class about 7–8 minutes to reflect on and answer these questions.

Core Concept 8.3

Most students need *coaching* and *structured opportunities to practice* their test reflection and analysis skills.

Small Group Reflection

After this personal, individual reflection activity, Ms. Walsh asked the students to get into their pre-assigned workgroups. Ms. Walsh established these groups based on the quality of interactions among certain students as well as their test performance. She wanted to ensure that the groups included students with a range of abilities so they

1) How do you think you performed on this test? _____ (possible score 1–3)

1	2	3
Not successful	Somewhat successful	Successful

How did you make that judgment?

_____

_____

2) How satisfied are you with your test grade? _____ (possible score 1–5).

1	2	3	4	5
Not satisfied at all	A little satisfied	Somewhat satisfied	Very satisfied	Extremely satisfied

3) What is (are) the main reason(s) why you got this test grade? (the WHY question!!)

_____

_____

4) What do you think you need to do to improve your next test grade? (the WHAT NOW question)

_____

_____

Figure 8.5 Example of a self-reflection form

could learn from each other. Before beginning this group activity, Ms. Walsh set some ground rules.

> "Now that you all have thought about your exams on your own, I would like you to talk in groups about questions number 3 and number 4 on the reflection form. Just remember a few rules. We are all here to help each other. If you did not perform as well as you would have liked, that is OK. You do not need to share at this point if you do not want to. But make sure you listen to what everyone has to say. If someone says something that interests you, then ask them about it. As you listen to each other, ask yourself whether you feel or experience similar things. The more you are able to have open conversations about these things, the greater the chance that you are going to learn some interesting things about how to improve. I also would like each of the groups to come up with a list of at least three things you feel are important to do as you prepare for the next test."

Ms. Walsh walked around the room to observe the group conversations. She made a point to listen carefully to the types of *attributions* (the WHY question) and *adaptive inferences* (the NOW WHAT question) that students expressed. She was particularly interested in listening to whether students focused on uncontrollable factors as the causes of their struggles (e.g., ability, test difficulty, etc.) or if they were beginning to THINK IN THE LANGUAGE OF STRATEGIES. Ms. Walsh then engaged the students in a brief group discussion about the primary themes and ideas that were discussed in the workgroups.

Conversations With Ms. Walsh – 8.2 Test Reflection Activities

During the reflection activity, both Ms. Walsh and Angie walked around the room. Angie found it particularly informative to hear the students talk about the tests. At times, she was impressed with what the students had to say. On the other hand, she was concerned with the negative beliefs and attitudes that other students exhibited. Angie was full of questions and wanted to bring them up to Ms. Walsh.

Angie: That was very cool. Some of the kids really got into a good conversation.

Ms. Walsh: I was not sure how well this would go, but I also thought it was pretty interesting. You could tell that this was a unique experience for many students. To be honest, I am not sure whether many of them would have ever reflected in this way if we had not prompted them to do so. I liked how some students really seemed to enjoy discussing these things. It seemed to be a validating experience for them; kind of like, "Hey, my thoughts and concerns actually matter."

Angie: But did you notice that some students chose not to say anything. They kind of just sat there and listened.

Ms. Walsh: I did, but I expected this. Most of those quiet students did not perform well. I suspect they were uncomfortable and perhaps did not know what to say. Regardless of whether they spoke up or not, I think they benefited from listening to the dialogue. I am not sure if you heard the conversation between Jack and Stephanie, but they both got a 79 on the test. Jack talked about how bad he was at taking tests and that he was just not good at memorizing facts and information. Stephanie agreed that she sometimes struggles with this too; but she kept shifting the conversation back to her attempts to use concept maps and other strategies to improve. It was interesting that she was so much more positive and strategic about her performance.

Angie: That is interesting. I agree that Stephanie seems to have a different mindset about these things. Do you think that students are just different? Some students are simply more motivated and positive?

Ms. Walsh: I used to think that way … you know, to label certain kids as lazy or unmotivated. But I am not sure if that is the right way to think about things. As I have been learning about SRL and motivation mindsets, I now think that much of what we see in kids is changeable. I think kids learn to become unmotivated and to exhibit negative beliefs and mindsets from the experiences that they have.

Angie: So you think that student beliefs about themselves and school has a major influence on how hard they try and how they react to tests?

Ms. Walsh: Yes, I do. Like I have stated many times recently, it is important that we get students to attribute their performance on tests and assignments to their own behaviors and strategies. When students get into this habit of reflecting on their successes or failures in the language of strategies, they are much more likely to focus on their strategic behaviors to improve. The differences between Stephanie and Jack perfectly illustrates this point. On one hand, Jack attributed his test grade to his poor ability and to "not being a good reader or writer." He also repeatedly stated that he had no chance of improving his grades and felt dumber than his classmates. Given his beliefs, I am very concerned about his motivation for the next test. On the other hand, Stephanie was like a beacon of hope. She received the identical grade but exhibited a much different attitude and way of thinking. Stephanie was primarily focused on improving her own performance. Further, when she answered the WHY question, she focused the entire conversation on the different tactics and strategies she used to study and how she needs to be get better at doing those things. Jack did not say anything in response to Stephanie when she was talking, but he was listening attentively to what she had to say. I think Stephanie's way of thinking made an impression on Jack.

Angie: I think you are right! I noticed that you also told the class to think about their test grades relative to their goals and prior test grades. You really seemed to emphasize that point. Why?

Ms. Walsh: I have come to realize that I may have been unintentionally getting students to focus on the wrong thing. I do not know if you ever noticed it or not, but when I handed back tests earlier in the year I would typically write the class test average on the board. My goal was to motivate students so that they could strive to get better.

Angie: So what is the big deal with that?

Ms. Walsh: By telling students about the class average, I naturally pushed them to think about their performance relative to others. Thus, students would ask themselves, "How well do I measure up against others?" rather than, "Am I improving or getting better?" For students who perform well, using norms is not much of an immediate problem. For students who struggle like Jack, however, they are likely to get pretty upset and stressed out. How motivated do you think Jack would be if he got a 71 on a test while also being told by us that the class average was an 88? Obviously, he would feel deflated or demoralized. So to answer your question, from here on out I am going to try very hard to not focus students' attention on how their classmates performed. I want them to focus exclusively on their own behaviors and individual progress. I want students to set goals and try to achieve their goals. I also want them to pay attention to patterns and trends in their own performance. If they learn to focus more on themselves and the specific strategies that they use to learn, it doesn't really matter how they stack up to their classmates.

Angie: But then you are suggesting that it is OK for students to accept less and not push themselves to be the best ... to be better than others. Is that right?

Ms. Walsh: That is not what I am really saying at all. Look at Stephanie. She set a goal of 85 for this past test. She did not reach her goal yet. Hopefully, she eventually does reach and surpass that goal. Once she does that, I would then encourage her to set a new goal, perhaps an 88 or 90. If she surpasses that goal then she can keep going up. I want all my students to strive for A's ... but I do not want them to worry and get stressed out if they perform worse than their classmates. That mindset or way of thinking won't help them improve. I want them to focus on their own their behavior and their own growth.

Angie: But is there a reason why you encourage them to focus on their goals and their prior test grades?

Ms. Walsh: Actually, yes. Doing this provides students with a more nuanced understanding of how they performed. If you look at Stephanie, she received a 74 and 72 on the two tests prior to the most recent one. Although she did not reach her goal of an 85, she did make progress – that is, she improved to a 79. By using these two evaluation standards, she will be much more likely to think things like, "I have not yet achieved my goal. But I am getting better." This is a much more positive and motivation-enhancing thing than saying, "I performed below most of the class again!"

Angie: Yeah, that part now makes sense. But I am still a little confused about why you seemed to focus so much on students' perceptions about the cause of their grades. Could you explain again?

Ms. Walsh: Well, the types of things to which students attribute their grades can have a big influence on how they feel and what they do next. By having students complete the Self-Reflection form and turn it into us, we will now have a better sense of how they think about success or failure. When I was walking around the room and briefly looked at student answers to the attribution question, I was a bit surprised at the range of answers that students were giving. Some students felt that they were incompetent, others blamed how hard the test was ... I even heard some students comment that I did not prepare them well enough for the test. All of these things are important because they represent what students think and believe. However, the problem is that many of these things are not under their control. A general rule of thumb is that when students feel they cannot change something or that they have no control over their learning, they tend to become demoralized and give up. I have a feeling that when we review these forms, we will see many responses that reflect students feeling demoralized and helpless. One professional goal that I have created for myself as a teacher is to strive to get students to THINK IN THE LANGUAGE OF STRATEGIES.

Angie: That is pretty deep. I have heard about having good mindsets and everything but I guess I really did not know what it meant. Something else I was thinking about was why did you have students reflect on their own and then in a group? Wouldn't some students be reluctant to share in a group?

Ms. Walsh: That is a good question. I wanted students to reflect on their own at first because self-reflection is a very personal and private thing. When students do not perform well, the last thing they want to do is share with others – they could be embarrassed or ashamed. But by giving them the option of sharing some of their thoughts in a group context, students can learn more positive ways of thinking from each other. This is why I don't think it is essential for all students to share in the group, at least initially anyway. They can still benefit by hearing what their classmates have to say. Like I said before, this is what I was beginning to see with Jack when he was listening to Stephanie's reflections.

Angie: Did you ask them to submit their self-reflection forms for the same reason why they turned in their Test Preparation worksheet?

Ms. Walsh: Yes. I may not have the time to closely read or review how all students answered the questions. But I think we have a better chance now of identifying whether students are focused on irrelevant factors as the causes of their grades or if they are in fact THINKING IN THE LANGUAGE OF STRATEGIES. I am also very interested in learning about what some students think they need to change or adapt in order to improve. If we can get a better sense of what students are thinking about, we can provide more useful feedback and guidance about how they can improve. When we meet as a class next week, I am going to give students the opportunity to meet with us to speak about some of these things.

Core Concept 8.4

Helping students make *strategic attributions* following performance and then guiding their thinking about *what* and *how to adapt* is a key component of developing SRLers.

Core Concept 8.5

When trying to apply SRL to classroom activities, start simple. Begin with one or two ideas until you feel comfortable and confident in what you are doing.

● ● ● ● ● ●

Concluding Thoughts

The central focus of this chapter was on Ms. Walsh and the adaptations she made to her test preparation and test review classroom activities. By using an SRL framework (like the one presented in Figure 8.1), Ms. Walsh was able to develop many ways to help students become more prepared, self-aware, and reflective about the testing process. She recognized the value of getting students to think more frequently about learning strategies and the need to shift their focus to their own behaviors, beliefs, and test grades. In Table 8.1, I summarize some of the key instructional tactics that Ms. Walsh used to engage students in cyclical, regulatory thinking and action.

Table 8.1 Ms. Walsh's instructional tactics to promote SRL skills in her students

Key challenges addressed in the classroom activity	Instructional tactics and approaches	SRL processes (corresponding chapter)
How did Ms. Walsh help students understand the characteristics, demands, and challenges of this specific test/exam?	• Test Preparation worksheet • Informal and formal prompts to engage in help seeking • Collaboration with peers as part of task analysis activities	• Task analysis (Ch. 4) • Strategic planning (Ch.4)
How did Ms. Walsh help students focus on and use the most relevant strategies to prepare for the test?	• Test Preparation worksheet • Study Plan	• Task and SRL focused strategies (Ch. 3)
In what ways did Ms. Walsh help students gather information about how they studied or prepared?	• Test Preparation worksheet • Study Plan worksheet • Self-Reflection form • SRL Graph • Feedback discussions	• Teacher feedback (Ch. 5) • Self-monitoring (Ch. 6)
How did Ms. Walsh help students think about and reflect on their performance in adaptive ways?	• Self-Reflection form • SRL Graph • Reference to Test Preparation and Study Plan worksheets • Feedback discussions • Adherence to principle of getting students to THINK IN LANGUAGE OF STRATEGIES	• Feedback (Ch. 5) • Self-monitoring (Ch.6) • Self-evaluation (Ch. 7) • Attributions (Ch. 7) • Adaptive inferences (Ch. 7)
How did Ms. Walsh help nurture student motivation?	• Self-Reflection form • SRL Graph • Feedback discussions • Adherence to principle of getting students to THINK IN LANGUAGE OF STRATEGIES	• Autonomy (Ch. 2) • Self-efficacy (Ch. 2) • Goal-setting (Ch. 4) • Attributions (Ch. 7)

An important question for all teachers to think about is, *"Should I engage students in test preparation and self-reflection activities or not?"* Although teachers can differ in their opinions or perspectives about this question, let me share some of the potential challenges that may emerge when introducing these types of activities in the classroom.

- Do these activities take time away from typical instruction? **Yes, to some degree**.
- Might the reflection activities lead to conversations that are critical of course assignments, the nature of tests, etc.? **Certainly, this is possible.**
- Is it easy to engage 25–30 students in an activity that is somewhat new to teachers and that may push students out of their comfort zone? **Of course not … engaging in classroom-wide self-reflection will take some time and practice.**
- Will most teachers automatically know about different studying and test preparation strategies that can lead to success? **Not always … teachers may need to brush up on these areas.**

These issues aside, most of you would probably agree with the premise that classroom tests will continue to be a common way for teachers to evaluate student learning. Even if you do not administer many tests in your class, the SRL framework and principles presented in this chapter are relevant to many other types of learning activities, such as essay writing, science projects, book reports, or oral presentations. In addition, I encourage you to use Figure 8.1 as a general guide to remind yourself about the key SRL-related questions to ask yourself and address when developing lesson plans.

● ● ● ● ●

References

Cleary, T. J., & Platten, P. (2013). Examining the correspondence between self-regulated learning and academic achievement: A case study analysis. *Education Research International*. 13 pages. doi: 10.1155/2013/272560.

Dunlosky, J., Rawson, K., Marsh, E., Nathan, M., & Willingham, D. (2013). Improving student's learning with effective learning techniques: Promising directions from cognitive and educational psychology. *Psychological Science in the Public Interest*, 14(1), 4–58.

Hattie, J. A. C., & Donoghue, G. M. (2016). Learning strategies: a synthesis and conceptual model. *Science of Learning*, 1, 16013. doi:10.1038/npjscilearn.2016.13.

Karabenick, S. A., & Berger, J. L. (2013). Help seeking as a self-regulated learning strategy. In H. Bembenutty, T. J. Cleary, and A. Kitsantas (Eds.), *Applications of self-regulated learning across disciplines: A tribute to Barry J. Zimmerman* (pp. 237–261). Charlotte, NC: Information Age Publishing.

Richardson, J. S., Robnolt, V. J., & Rhodes, J. A. (2010). A history of study skills: Not hot, but not forgotten. *Reading Improvement*, 27(2), 111–123.

Weinstein, C. E., & Acee, T. W. (2013). Helping college students become more strategic and self-regulated learners. In H. Bembenutty, T. J. Cleary, and A. Kitsantas (Eds.), *Applications of self-regulated learning across disciplines: A tribute to Barry J. Zimmerman* (pp. 197–236). Charlotte, NC: Information Age Publishing.

9

Teaching SRL Skills: Classroom-Based Lessons and Activities

Teach the children so it will not be necessary to teach the adults.
—Abraham Lincoln

 Chapter Snapshot

Chapter 9 focuses on applying SRL and motivation practices to classroom-based lessons and projects. Specifically, I examine how a ninth-grade life science teacher, Ms. Johnson, incorporates SRL concepts into her two-day lesson on natural selection. To illustrate her SRL classroom innovations, I present a conversation between Ms. Johnson and one of her colleagues and with the school principal. Although this case study does not depict actual, real-life conversations, the lesson plan represents a variation of an authentic science lesson plan presented elsewhere (Cleary et al., 2018).

Reader Reflection – 9.1 Classroom-Based Lessons

Think back to a recent class session when you asked your students to engage in some type of activity (e.g., science laboratory exercise, a small group reciprocal teaching reading activity, a mathematics problem-solving practice session, etc.). It does not matter if the activity involves students working individually or in small groups. As you reflect on this activity, consider the extent to which you:

- Helped students develop a clear plan regarding how to complete the activity

- Enabled students to track their behaviors or performance during the activity

- Guided students to evaluate and reflect on their behaviors or performance on the activity

- Motivated students to more fully engage in the activity

Introduction

There are many instructional methods and strategies that teachers use within their classrooms to optimize student learning, such as direct instruction approaches (e.g., modeling, explicit teaching), inquiry-based methods, and interactive or collaborative approaches (e.g., reciprocal teaching, cooperative learning groups). For example, Ms. Martinez, a 5th grade elementary school teacher, likes to use direct instruction to teach basic skills in mathematics, but shifts to a reciprocal teaching framework when addressing reading skills. Conversely, a middle school social studies teacher, Ms. Lemme, emphasizes the use of case studies and concept mapping as well as some types of experiential methods (e.g., field trips) to help students learn. Finally, at the high school level, Ms. Johnson has become fond of using inquiry-based learning in her science lessons as well as instruction that integrates direct instruction with collaborative forms of learning.

My objective in this chapter is not to emphasize one instructional strategy approach over another, nor is it to address all potential applications of SRL relative to these instructional approaches or specific content areas (see Butler, Schnellert, & Perry, 2017; Cleary, 2015, and DiBenedetto, 2018, for additional illustrations). My goal is simple. To present an exemplar case study that illustrates how teachers can embed SRL and motivation principles within a complex lesson plan. Similar to Chapter 8, I demonstrate how teachers can infuse an integrated set of SRL processes during authentic classroom activities.

Linking SRL to Classroom-Based Projects and Activities

Ms. Johnson is a 9th grade biology teacher in an urban high school who has approximately nine years of teaching experience. Like many science teachers, Ms. Johnson uses lab experiments to help students engage in the scientific method and to learn about core science concepts. One of her favorite lab exercises involves the topic of natural selection. Her lesson plan integrates elements of direct instruction strategies with collaborative learning and experiential instructional strategies (see Figure 9.1). This lesson also represents a modification of an authentic lesson developed by Caroline Gergel, a biology teacher at a high school in Virginia (see Cleary et al., 2018). The key objective of this chapter is to illustrate how Ms. Johnson adapted her lesson plan to incorporate SRL and motivation principles.

Although Ms. Johnson was pleased with the overall structure and context of the lab exercise, she has begun to question its effectiveness. Many of the students were not as engaged with the material as she had expected. She thought that the bunny activity (use of beans) and the geometric design activity would motivate all of her students, but unfortunately, this was not the case. Further, several students had difficulty directing their own behaviors across the different parts of the lab exercise, even though Ms. Johnson gave clear and explicit directions. Finally, the students did not deeply or strategically approach the various activities within the lesson, resulting in many of them getting "stuck" at several points during the lesson.

Ms. Johnson expressed some of her frustration about the lesson with one of her colleagues, Mr. Filipo. After listening to Ms. Johnson vent, he smiled and nodded reassuringly because he had also encountered a similar situation. Mr. Filipo talked with her about his own struggles with his students and shared some strategies that he used effectively to "reach" students (see Conversations with Ms. Johnson).

Teaching SRL Skills: Classroom-Based Lessons and Activities

141

Natural Selection Lesson Plan – Day 1

- *Pre-lab activities* – Students read a text about bunnies living in an environment where having fur is adaptive; students answer questions to assess prior knowledge of genetics.
- *Modeling* – Teacher and a student model lab procedures, with an emphasis on data recording of alleles for presence and absence of fur (using pairs of red and white beans).
- *Guided practice* – Students go through lab procedures and record data for one bunny generation. Teacher provides guided practice (scaffolding, hints, feedback).
- *Independent practice* – Students engage in independent practice to complete data tables across several bunny generations.
- *Analysis* – Students graph results and interpret data.

Natural Selection Lesson Plan – Day 2

- *Assessment* – Teacher administers quiz to examine student learning from Day 1.
- *Video of Galapagos species* – Teacher shows 10-minute video about natural selection for Galapagos species to reinforce premise that natural selection results in gene pool change over time.
- *Darwin mini-activity* – Teacher provides explicit instruction in Darwinism to further promote the idea that visible traits represent the interaction of two alleles.
- *Geometric illustration* – Teacher prompts students to use pie chart about mouse alleles to create a geometric design of a mouse with different alleles.
- *Text reading* – Students read text descriptions of different species with either beneficial or maladaptive traits that affect evolution.

Figure 9.1 Ms. Johnson's original lesson plan for natural selection

---

Conversations With Ms. Johnson – 8.1 Advice from a Colleague

Mr. Filipo: I hear what you are saying about the challenge of getting students to engage more fully in their work during class. To tell you the truth, I was at my wits end. But after I took an honest look at some of my old teaching habits, I really felt that that I needed to do some things differently. It is not always perfect or easy, but I think I have a much better handle on how to motivate students and to get them to be more proactive and strategic in their thinking – well at least some of the time.

Ms. Johnson: Really? What do you do?

Mr. Filipo: Well, it is not one thing per se. It is more of an approach that includes different things. Whenever I engage students in some activity during class, I now think about several things that I never really focused on. Well, even before I get to that, I guess the most important thing I do is make sure that I completely understand what the learning activity requires of my students.

Ms. Johnson: I am not sure what you mean. We develop the activities for our classes, so of course we know what they are about.

Mr. Filipo: I agree. But what I mean is do you ever reflect on the nuances or specific challenges that most students will likely encounter? Will certain parts of the activity require them to stop and think, or to reflect? Are there specific strategies that they can learn that

Teaching SRL Skills: Classroom-Based Lessons and Activities

will help them to complete different parts of the activity? Will students likely get confused because the activity involves many parts or procedures?

Ms. Johnson: Well, I think about these things at times, but not just how you said it. But why is dissecting an activity in this way so important?

Mr. Filipo: At a teacher workshop that I recently attended, I learned about something called self-regulated learning (SRL). SRL refers to a bunch of skills and ways of thinking that helps people direct and control their behaviors as they learn. A key point was that teachers can most effectively teach SRL in the classroom when these SRL ideas are directly embedded in their lesson plans and activities. You were just talking before about your frustration with your students – they often were unaware of what they were doing or how to improve; they didn't really "get" what the lesson was all about; and they were often not strategic when completing class activities. I think you also said that they also tend to give up easily and disengage from the activity. I had to smile when I heard you say these things because they all seem to directly relate to this concept of SRL.

Ms. Johnson: I guess that sounds interesting, but I don't have the time to devote to adding more things to my class activities. I am too busy during class.

Mr. Filipo: I don't know whether this will help you, but I made a copy of a simple instructional guide that I read about in a book on SRL. This guide involves a series of questions that teachers can use to get themselves focused on things that are critical for students to think about and do when learning. I often use these questions to help me structure my learning activities. The goal is to get students to become more cognitively engaged during learning – you know, things like thinking ahead, planning, and reflecting on what they are doing. I gave this prompt to Ms. Walsh. She uses it to guide her test preparation activities during social studies class.

Ms. Johnson: But that guide seems to relate to test preparation. How does that relate to the things I do in my class?

Mr. Filipo: I'll tell you what, come to my classroom during our prep time and I will show you what I mean. I think it will be fairly easy to customize this guide to what you need.

Core Concept 9.1

Successful application of SRL to a classroom context involves a *flexible, fluid approach* rather than a rigid application of rules and procedures.

Core Concept 9.2

Before you can infuse SRL principles into class lesson plans and activities, you need to clearly understand the demands, expectations, and nuances of those activities.

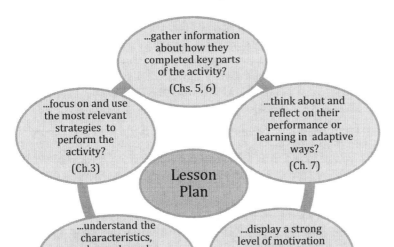

Figure 9.2 Instructional prompt to guide SRL-infused lesson plan

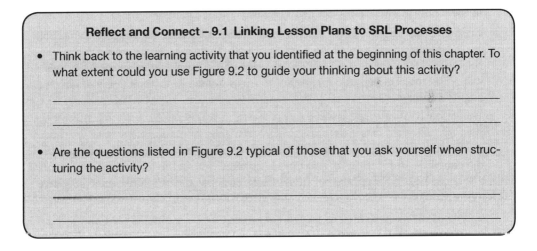

Merging Classroom Instruction and SRL Principles

Before reading this section, please read and address the questions in Reflect and Connect exercise 9.1. Ms. Johnson was intrigued by her conversation with Mr. Filipo. She was particularly interested in the part about how SRL concepts helped him develop more effective lesson plans and activities for his class. But she was also skeptical. After all, it seemed like

Natural Selection Lesson Plan – Day 1

- *Pre-lab activities* – students read a text about bunnies living in an environment where having fur is adaptive; students answer questions to assess prior knowledge of genetics; **students make predictions about the expected changes in allele frequency before beginning the lab (forethought thinking).**

- *Modeling* – teacher and a student model lab procedures, with an emphasis on data recording of alleles for presence and absence of fur (using pairs of red and white beans).

- *Guided practice* – **students estimate the number of alleles to be counted before data collection (forethought thinking);** students go through lab procedures and record data for one bunny generation; teacher provides guided practice (scaffolding, hints, feedback).

- *Independent practice* – students engage in independent practice to complete data tables across several bunny generations; **students complete a monitoring form to track their use of specific strategies during the bean activity (self-monitoring); teacher circulates the room to provide feedback to students about the quality of their behaviors and answers (efficacy enhancement feedback).**

- *Analysis* – students graph results and interpret data.

Natural Selection Lesson Plan – Day 2

- *Assessment* – teacher administers quiz to examine student learning from Day 1; **teacher reviews quiz to emphasize points of mastery (efficacy enhancement).**

- *Video of Galapagos species* – teacher shows 10-minute video about natural selection for Galapagos species to reinforce premise that natural selection results in gene pool change over time; **teacher enhances the video with a theme song of a popular video game that most of her students enjoy and that relates to the challenge of survival (interest enhancement).**

- *Darwin mini-activity* – teacher provides explicit instruction in Darwinism to further promote the idea that visible traits represent the interaction of two alleles; **students make predictions about changes in trait frequency before beginning the activity (forethought); students answer two self-reflection questions after assessing accuracy of their predications (attributions and adaptive inferences).**

- *Geometric illustration* – teacher prompts students to use pie chart about mouse alleles to create a geometric design of a mouse with different alleles; **teacher gives students a checklist of the key principles to keep in mind as they proceed through this component (self-monitoring).**

- *Text reading* – students read text descriptions of different specifies with either beneficial or maladaptive traits that affect evolution.

Figure 9.3 Ms. Johnson's SRL – enhanced lesson plan for natural selection
*Note: Bolded text reflects SRL and motivation enhancements.

Teaching SRL Skills: Classroom-Based Lessons and Activities   145

a lot of work and like most teachers, she was busy trying to just keep up with covering the curriculum, grading student tests and homework, etc. Fortunately, Mr. Filipo was a good friend and has become a staunch advocate of merging SRL principles into classroom instruction. He was also willing to spend some time guiding her through this process.

Together, they extended and refined the original natural selection lesson plan. Given that this was Ms. Johnson's first attempt at implementing SRL into a lesson plan, they felt that the best course of action would be to focus on only a few elements from the SRL instructional guide (Figure 9.2). She could then expand what she does over time. Ms. Johnson decided to focus on structuring the learning activities to help students:

- become more motivated
- increase their self-awareness through self-monitoring
- become more strategic and self-reflective thinkers.

Given that Ms. Johnson had not yet administered the original natural selection lesson to one of her class sections, she was excited with the opportunity to deliver the revised lesson (see Figure 9.3; Cleary et al. 2018). Ms. Johnson was also a type of teacher who was very open to feedback and was willing to adjust or change her instructional approach if it would help her students. Thus, she asked her principal, Mr. Sheffield, to observe and provide feedback about the revised lesson. Mr. Sheffield had recently observed Ms. Johnson's original lab exercise but agreed to observe her again because he was curious about the changes that she made. He was particularly intrigued by the potential influence of SRL; a concept that he had recently been hearing a lot about (see Conversations With Ms. Johnson).

Conversations With Ms. Johnson – 8.2 Perspectives of a Principal

Mr. Sheffield was excited to observe Ms. Johnson's revised lesson. Although he had planned on only observing the classroom on Day 1 of the lesson, he decided to come back on Day 2 because he was intrigued by Day 1 SRL instructional practices. A few days after the observation, Mr. Sheffield arranged for a meeting with Ms. Johnson to talk about the lesson. Their conversation was organized into three conceptual areas or talking points.

Talking Point #1: Getting Students to Self-Evaluate and Reflect

Mr. Sheffield: Jen, I really liked your lesson. Like I told you after the first observation, you included some great content. But I noticed that you did some things differently. Also, many of the students were very engaged and reflective as they went through the activities.

Ms. Johnson: Thanks.

Mr. Sheffield: Something that really intrigued me was the number of times that you asked students to predict or to make hypotheses. Why did you do that?

Ms. Johnson: I have been talking with Mr. Filipo, who also does some of these things with his students. One of the things I have learned is that getting students to set goals or make predictions before they do something will help them evaluate how they are learning. That is, it helps them to ask themselves, "How well I am learning?" or "Was I correct?" One of the struggles that I have had in recent years is getting my students to become more aware of what they are doing as they complete my science labs. Many students seem to operate on autopilot, without ever stopping to think and evaluate how well they are learning. I asked them to predict a lot because I want them to stop and analyze things more … to become more like a mini-detective or scientist.

Mr. Sheffield: You mentioned self-regulated learning. What does SRL have to do with making predictions?

Ms. Johnson: I wouldn't say making predictions is the same thing as SRL, but getting students to predict can prompt them to become more regulatory in their thinking. When students make predictions or hypotheses about something, those predictions become the benchmarks or standards against which students can ask, "Was I correct?" or "How did I do?" So by having my students make several predictions throughout the lab, I was naturally getting them to continually pause, self-assess, and then identify ways to improve.

Mr. Sheffield: What you just said is similar to what I meant about your students being very engaged and reflective as they learned. Were there other things that you did to get students to reflect on their learning?

Ms. Johnson: Yes, the data table aspect of the lab also involved student evaluation. On Day 1, I had students collaborate with their classmates to create their own data tables. I then provided them with an exemplary data table. By giving them an exemplary data table, I prompted them to ask themselves, "Was my data table appropriate? Why or Why not?" A big part of SRL instruction is getting students to make judgments about how well they are learning and then nudging them to fix things that may go awry.

Mr. Sheffield: Hmmm … that is great. I think I am beginning to see your thinking now. When you had them make predictions or, in this case, when you gave them the exemplary data table, you were ultimately giving them the standard or benchmark for evaluating themselves.

Ms. Johnson: Exactly. It is very difficult to get students to think and reflect adaptively unless they have a clear standard or benchmark in their head.

Mr. Sheffield: So that is how you addressed reflection. I like it.

Ms. Johnson: Actually, there were a couple of other things I did to get students to dig a bit deeper as they reflected. In addition to helping them figure out how well they were doing, I prompted them to reflect on why they might have performed that way and what they needed to do to learn more effectively. I am not sure if you noticed this, but after my students evaluated the accuracy of their predictions on the Darwin activity, I asked them to answer two questions, "Why was my prediction wrong/correct?" and "What do I need to do to improve?" We then talked as a class about these things. These two questions address what SRL researchers call causal attributions and adaptive inferences. By explicitly talking about these things, I was helping to guide students' judgments and reactions about their learning.

Mr. Sheffield: Very nice. It is almost as if you are using theory and research to guide your instruction.

Ms. Johnson: I had not thought about it like that, but the SRL theory that I have been learning about seems to tie in nicely to the things I am now doing in the classroom.

Teaching SRL Skills: Classroom-Based Lessons and Activities | **147**

Core Concept 9.3

Getting your students into the habit of *pausing* and *reflecting* about their learning is a subtle yet powerful way to enhance their learning and success.

Talking Point #2: Getting Students to Become More Self-Aware

Mr. Sheffield: I am really impressed with how you got your students to self-reflect so much. It was so natural and seemed to require minimal effort on your part. Another thing I really liked about the lesson was that you were able to get the students to be very active. I couldn't tell exactly what they were doing all of the time, but on several occasions it looked like they were recording and writing things down. What was the purpose of having them do that?

Ms. Johnson: Yes, I had the students monitor several things that they were doing during the lab. Obviously, a big part of this lesson was getting students to use a data recording table to keep track of the alleles during the bean activity. So the use of this monitoring table was designed to help students learn about a key aspect of the scientific process — the value of systematically recording data.

Mr. Sheffield: I get that part, but you seemed to get them to monitor other things too, right?

Ms. Johnson: Yes … a couple of different things. Like I said before, as part of the reflection activity, I had them evaluate the accuracy of their predictions, the causes of their performance, and things they needed to improve. I had them write down their answers to these questions because I wanted them to have a record of the things they thought about when completing the activity (see Figure 9.4). I am hopeful that the act of writing things down further reinforced to them the importance of pausing, self-assessing, and figuring out what to do next. I also think that by having students self-record, they will be able to gain a better understanding of their own misconceptions or errors in their thinking.

Mr. Sheffield: I love it! Getting students to discover or gain insights about their own thinking is very important. Did you ever think about having small group activities or an overall class discussion to review their specific answers to these questions? Could that be helpful?

Ms. Johnson: I had not really thought about it at this point. But now that you mention it, I think it might have been helpful. In thinking back to those parts of the lessons, I had a chance to review some of their answers. But honestly, I did not have enough time to do this. Perhaps having them break up into small groups to talk about these things and then having me lead a brief discussion at the end of the lesson could be a way to directly explore and challenge student patterns of thinking and behaviors.

Mr. Sheffield: That is a great idea! I think you could also collect their monitoring sheets to get a closer look at what students had to say. This may be a useful way for you to better understand how students who struggle in your class truly think and react during the lesson.

Ms. Johnson: That is true. Although I may not be able to go through all of the students' answers, I could focus my attention on those who seemed to struggle. Another monitoring activity that I included in this lesson, and one that I now incorporate into all of my class activities, was having students keep track of their behaviors and use of strategies. For example, as students completed the bean activity across several bunny generations, I had them track a few important behaviors that are relevant to the activity (see Figure 9.5). This was a very simple monitoring form, but one that I think could have a big effect. This form was designed to get students to become more aware of a few behaviors that I feel are critical to this activity. In a sense, I was trying to get the students to become more aware and in tune to their own behaviors.

Mr. Sheffield: I think that is another wonderful idea! But I did not see you talk to students about that particular form. Is that something that they only do on their own?

Ms. Johnson: My intention was to address it. Like I said before, I kind of ran out of time. The difficult thing with infusing some of these SRL ideas into my classroom is that I cannot do everything. As I get more familiar and efficient in doing these things, perhaps I can engage students in a more efficient way. The good news is that by having students monitor their strategic behaviors during the lesson, many of them seemed to become more aware of what they were doing. It also gets them to THINK IN THE LANGUAGE OF STRATEGIES.

Mr. Sheffield: THINK IN THE LANGUAGE OF STRATEGIES? What do you mean?

Ms. Johnson: This is just a catchy phrase to remind myself about the importance of getting students to think about being purposeful and strategic as they approach and complete learning activities. Too often, students focus on grades and outcomes. What I have been learning is that getting students to focus on the process – that is, their behaviors and actions linked to success on that activity, is of greater importance.

Mr. Sheffield: What is really amazing about all of this is that I would not have noticed some of these nuances if we had not debriefed about the lesson. It is almost as if these SRL principles are naturally embedded within the flow of the lesson. They are kind of hidden or covert things that overlap directly with the content that you are trying to teach them.

Ms. Johnson: Yes, I agree. I could see what Mr. Filipo meant when he told me that over time his instruction and the SRL principles become difficult to separate. They are really one and the same.

Pause and reflect questions	Student responses
1. Was my prediction of the expected change in trait frequency correct?	
2. If my prediction was not correct, why do I think the prediction was off? What happened?	
3. Is there anything I need to figure out or learn better?	

Figure 9.4 Self-monitoring worksheet of predictions

Did I remember to do the following things?	Yes	No
1. Double check the accuracy of my data recording?		
2. Check whether my predictions were correct?		
3. Ask questions of my classmates or teacher when confused?		

Figure 9.5 Self-monitoring worksheet used during bean activity

---

Core Concept 9.4

Encouraging students to *monitor their strategic behaviors* during learning will often increase their awareness about the link between these actions and performance.

Talking Point #3: Getting Students to Become More Motivated to Learn

Mr. Sheffield: Another thing that I noticed was that your students were very engaged and motivated. Like you said before, getting your students to make several predictions really seemed to get them thinking and more engaged. But there seemed to be more to it than that. They were much more animated and interested in the lesson than students from your other section. Was this group of students just different or was it something else?

Ms. Johnson: Actually, I am very happy that you noticed that. For a long time, I had struggled with how to motivate my students to want to learn more. I hate to admit this but I was not very good at motivating students. I would try to praise them and reinforce positive behaviors, which seemed to work OK for some. But I was never able to get most of my students really "into it."

Mr. Sheffield: So what did you do differently?

Ms. Johnson: That is the funny thing … there was not ONE thing. I still do not think it is easy thing to do for all students, but this is what I did in the lesson. I tried to target student beliefs and perceptions. From what I have learned about SRL and motivation, the ways in which students think and feel about themselves, their teachers, and their classroom environment has a big effect on how hard they try and whether they will persist. So, when I design lesson plans, I now think about how I can enhance student self-efficacy, how I can make a lesson more fun and interesting, how I can give students more freedom to make choices during learning, and how I can reinforce positive, inspiring mindsets.

Mr. Sheffield: Interesting … so how did you address all of those things in the lesson?

Ms. Johnson: Well, I am just learning to do this, so I was not able to address everything that I could have. But I did target student self-efficacy, interest, and strategic attributions. To target each of these beliefs, I first asked myself what I specifically needed to do during the lesson to promote that belief. For example, when it came to self-efficacy, the key thing

150 Teaching SRL Skills: Classroom-Based Lessons and Activities

is to provide students with frequent opportunities to demonstrate success. As part of the lesson, each time that students evaluated their predictions and upon receiving feedback about the Day 2 quiz and the quality of their Day 1 homework, I attempted to emphasize the specific areas that they had mastered and one or two areas in need of improvement. Developing greater interest in the lesson was fairly straightforward. Students will often show greater interest in activities when the activities are fun and when they relate to some aspect of students' lives. By conveying the process of natural selection across different species and through using different modalities (video, bean activity, making a geometric design, etc.) I think I was able to sustain their interest and attention. But what really seemed to have an effect on their engagement was embedding a theme song from a popular video game into the instructional video about the Galapagos species. The students love the song and really got them into it – at least for that part of the lesson anyway.

Mr. Sheffield: Huh ... that is amazing that you were able to target all of those things in a lesson. It also did not really seem to take much time away, if at all, from the lesson.

Ms. Johnson: To be honest, it was not as easy as it sounds. I had to really think through some of these ideas about motivation. But once I started to actually target these beliefs it became a lot easier. What was interesting was that I never realized just how important student beliefs and perceptions were to getting kids to want to learn. I am now much more mindful and strategic about how I give feedback and the specific things that I say to students. Although I do not think every student was highly motivated during the lesson, I know that some students definitely became more invested in the lesson. I will keep tinkering and trying to figure out what each student needs in order to experience greater motivation.

Core Concept 9.5

Motivating students to learn is not a one-time event. It is a *dynamic, on-going process* of helping to nurture and cultivate adaptive student beliefs and self-perceptions.

Concluding Thoughts

Across all content areas and grade levels, teachers use various instructional approaches and learning activities to enhance student learning. As I illustrated in this chapter, infusing SRL instruction into typical classroom routines and practices is not only possible, it can greatly shape how students think, feel, and act during the lesson. As you consider how to infuse SRL principles into your instructional approaches and lesson plans, I recommend that you use Figure 9.2 to guide your thinking.

There are many ways in which you can promote student planning, monitoring, strategy use, and self-evaluation (see Table 9.1 to identify how Ms. Johnson linked science lab activities to SRL). Just remember that targeting these SRL processes should not be viewed as "extra" things beyond your regular instruction; rather, SRL instruction and content-area instruction should be naturally intertwined and integrated.

I am also hopeful that you are beginning to recognize the value in designing classroom activities that spark student interest and that can give them multiple opportunities to judge and evaluate success. Ultimately, when classroom activities enable

Table 9.1 Ms. Johnson's approach to promoting SRL skills during a science investigation

Key challenges addressed in the science lesson	Instructional tactics and approaches	SRL processes (corresponding chapter in SRL book)
How did Ms. Johnson help students understand the characteristics, demands, and challenges of this specific classroom activity?	• Modeling and guided practice • Pre-task reading activity • Knowledge test	• Task analysis (Ch. 4)
How did Ms. Johnson help students focus on and use the most relevant strategies to prepare for the lab?	• Monitoring worksheets (Figures 9.4 and 9.5) • Classroom discussion about strategic thinking	• Task and SRL focused strategies (Ch. 3)
In what ways did Ms. Johnson help students gather information about how they completed the lab exercise?	• Monitoring forms (data recording, behaviors, SRL processes) • Prediction accuracy • Feedback discussions	• Feedback (Ch. 5) • Self-monitoring (Ch. 6)
How did Ms. Johnson help students think about and reflect on their performance in adaptive ways?	• Multiple prediction activities • Monitoring responses to self-reflection questions	• Self-monitoring (Ch.6) • Self-evaluation (Ch. 7) • Attributions (Ch. 7) • Adaptive inferences (Ch. 7)
How did Ms. Johnson help to enhance student motivation?	• Prediction activities • Self-reflection activities • Enhancing task features and modalities of instruction • Efficacy and interest enhancement	• Self-efficacy (Ch. 2) • Interest (Ch. 2) • Attributions (Ch. 7)

students to become more interested, engaged, and strategic as they complete those activities, students will often experience greater success (Cleary et al., 2017; Hidi & Ainley, 2008; Wentzel, 2012).

In closing, my exclusive focus on a specific science lesson in this chapter should not limit or restrict your thinking about how SRL can be applied in classrooms. All of the SRL principles that I emphasized in this chapter (and in Chapter 8 for that matter) are also applicable to reading, writing, and mathematics lessons as well as classroom activities in other content areas, such foreign language or social studies (see Butler et al., 2017, Cleary, 2015; DiBenedetto, 2018). The key things to remember are to enhance your understanding of the core components of the learning activities or assignments for your class, and to identify how SRL and motivation principles can be integrated within those activities.

●●●●●

References

Butler, D. L., Schnellert, L., & Perry, N. E. (2017). *Developing self-regulating learners.* Upper Saddle River, NJ: Pearson Education, Inc.

Cleary, T. J. (Ed.). (2015). *Self-regulated learning interventions with at-risk youth: Enhancing adaptability, performance, and well-being.* Washington, DC: American Psychological Association.

Cleary, T. K., Peters-Burton, E., Gergel, C., & Willet, K. (2018). Applications of cyclical self-regulated learning principles to science contexts. In M. K. DiBenedetto (Ed.), *Connecting self-regulated learning and performance with instruction across high school content areas.* New York: Springer

DiBenedetto, M. K. (Ed.). (2018). *Connecting self-regulated learning and performance with instruction across high school content areas.* New York: Springer.

Hidi, S., & Ainley, M. (2008). Interest and self-regulation: Relationship between two variables that influence learning. In D. H. Schunk and B. J. Zimmerman (Eds.). *Motivation and self-regulated learning: Theory, research, and applications* (pp. 77–109). New York: Lawrence Erlbaum Associates.

Wentzel, K. (2012). Commentary: Socio-cultural contexts, social competence, and engagement at school. In S. L. Christenson, A. L. Reschly, & C. Wylie (Eds.). *Handbook of research on student engagement* (pp. 479–488). New York: Springer.

Final Thoughts ●●●●●

Writing this book was an exciting and satisfying endeavor for me given that SRL concepts have consumed so much of my attention and energy over the past two decades. SRL is one of those "mega concepts" that is applicable to virtually any context that involves learning and performance. What made writing this book even more special was the potential to influence the thinking and actions of teachers – a group of professionals whom I greatly respect and admire. It is my hope that a few themes espoused in this book resonated at a core level with you and served as a source of inspiration to create SRL-supportive and motivation-enhancing classroom environments.

At its core, this book was about you and your teaching. As I have previously stated, the SRL principles and themes presented in this book should not be viewed as a set of "add on" or "extra" things you need to do in the classroom. It is best to view SRL instruction within the framework of your typical classroom routines, practices, and instructional approaches. Thus, SRL instruction and your typical content-area instruction should be intertwined, not separate. They should naturally inform and complement each other.

It is also important to remember that, as a teacher, you should not feel that you have to address all processes within the SRL cyclical feedback loop (e.g., goals, plans, monitoring, attributions, etc.) in all teaching situations or for all learning activities. Take it slowly. Closely examine the demands of your assignments and classroom lessons and try to become more mindful of the challenges that your students experience. After doing these things, ask yourself, *"Which SRL principles would be most helpful for my students to learn in this specific situation as they complete that particular activity?"* I certainly am not minimizing the importance of engaging students in the full, cyclical feedback loop. Getting students to think ahead and plan, to monitor themselves during learning, and to reflect adaptively on their learning are all important. I am simply trying to emphasize that Rome was not built in a day. Becoming proficient in teaching SRL skills will take some time and practice. Therefore, focus on the constructs that you feel would be most helpful to you and your students, and then build from there.

In closing, I want to leave you with a few final thoughts that capture some of the "big" SRL ideas that may be of particular value to you as a teacher.

- Get students to THINK IN THE LANGUAGE OF STRATEGIES. I used this phrase in the book's subtitle and emphasized it in most chapters. In using this phrase, I am not advocating that we simply want students to think about strategies in a general way or to identify one or two strategies to use when learning. Rather, I am trying to call your attention to the fact that getting students to think about strategies is relevant and important across all phases of task engagement – *before* students begin an assignment, *during* their completion of the assignment, and *after* students receive feedback or complete the assignment. It is also important to not only get students to use strategies when completing a learning activity, but to also have them reflect on *when, where, why,* and *how* to use and adapt them as needed.
- Get students to generate their own feedback. Although teacher feedback is critical to student success, students can play some role in the feedback generation process. When developing learning activities, assignments, or projects, try to help your

students monitor select aspects of activities that *you believe* are most critical for them to focus on. In addition to helping increase student awareness and mindfulness about personal strengths and weaknesses, self-monitoring can naturally stimulate students to answer critical questions about themselves, such as, "Am I learning well?," "Am I effectively using the strategy that I was taught in class?," or "Are there parts of this assignment or activity that are confusing or challenging?"

- Give students structured opportunities to practice *self-reflection*. All people naturally think about and reflect on their grades and performance outcomes. However, simply having general reflective thoughts is not the same thing as engaging in a systematic process of self-reflection. Throughout this book, I offered several ideas regarding how teachers can encourage self-reflection in the classroom. Regardless of the specific approach to reflection that you might use, it is important to help students frequently engage in self-reflection and to do so in a structured way. Specifically, I encourage you to prompt your students to focus on *self-standards* (goals, prior performance) when evaluating a grade and to think about the *strategic causes* of their successes or failures. It is also relevant for you to provide students with opportunities to express and share their self-perceptions and reactions to performance with you or their classmates. Then give them guidance about how to adapt, refine, or tweak their strategic approaches to school.

As you might have noticed, I love all things SRL. I believe it is one of the most important set of skills that students can learn because of the positive effects it can have on student learning, performance, and development during K-12, college, and beyond.

I hope you found this book to be enjoyable and relevant to your role as teacher. Please reach out to me if you have any questions about SRL or its many applications to schools.

Index ● ● ● ● ●

adaptive inferences 73, 76, 103, 133
adaptive reflection skills 117
anxiety 75, 104
attributions 73, 76, 103, 110–115, 133
autonomy 21, 29–34, 90, 95, 98, 99
avoidance 55, 75; *see also* failure, perceptions;
    helplessness

Bandura, A. 22–23
beliefs/perceptions, student 20, 83–84,
    102–104
Butler, Deborah 57

calibration accuracy 91
career ambitions, student 27, 28
case studies: Ms. Johnson (teacher) 140–151;
    Ms. Walsh (teacher) 125–137
challenges 8–9
characteristics of SRL 9–11
cognitive strategies 39
competence *see* mastery; self-efficacy
competition and performance pressure 105
complex tasks, breaking down 23–24
confidence *see* self-efficacy
controllability 112–115
corrective feedback 75–76

Dead Poets Society 20
Deci, Edward 29
delayed teacher feedback 82–83
demonstrated success, and self-efficacy
    23–25, 90, 103
direct coaching 116
Dweck, Carol 31–32

effective feedback 80
effort attributions 114
emotional reactions 39; and attribution 111,
    113; and self-monitoring 90, 95–96; and
    self-reflection 102
empathy 30
environmental restructuring 39, 41
evaluation *see* self-evaluation; tests

failure, perceptions 33, 108–109, 113; *see also*
    controllability
feedback, teacher 71–86; and self-evaluation/
    reflection 109, 116–117; on tests 130–131;
    see also self-monitoring

feedback dialogue 84, 116
feedback loop 12, 73, 88, 117
films, student–teacher dynamics 20, 22
fixed mindset 32–33, 123
forethought 12–13, 55–56, 68

goals 39, 54, 62–66, 106, 107–108, 109–110;
    see also normative standards
grades 72, 104–105; prior grades 106, 107,
    109–110
Graham, Steven 43
graphing 92, 96, 107–108, 131–132
group reflection 117, 132–136
growth mindset 21, 22, 31–33, 115
guided practice 45, 141

Harris, Karen 38, 41, 43, 47–48
Hattie, J. 74
help seeking 39, 116
helplessness 11, 33, 75, 113; *see also*
    avoidance; failure, perceptions; stress

instructional strategies 140
instrumentality/value 21, 22, 25, 26–28, 95
intelligence, perceptions 32, 55, 74–75, 105
interest 21, 26–27, 95

KISS method 94

learning activities 11; analysis 46; key
    components 81; and three-phase model
    15–16; *see also* task analysis
lesson plans, science 139–145; SRL-enhanced
    142, 145
listening, active 30

mastery 22, 23–25
mathematics 67, 72, 76, 77–78, 94; and
    mistakes 33; and task analysis 57; and
    task strategies 41, 45–46
metacognitive skills 11
modeling 44–45, 141
monitoring *see* self-monitoring
motivation 10, 19–36, 94–95, 103, 105, 108,
    149–150; prompts 59; and teacher
    feedback 83
movies, student–teacher dynamics 20, 22
multiple practice formats 45

Index

normative standards 106, 107, 109, 135

opportunities, performance 23–25
outcome goals 64, 65

Parcells, Bill 9, 23
peers as co-facilitators 117
performance information *see* feedback, teacher; tests
performance opportunities 23–25
performance outcomes 92, 95–98
performance phase 13
personal goals *see* goals
personal responsibility *see* autonomy; responsibility, teacher; self-monitoring
personal/prior knowledge 39, 41
persuasion 22
planning 42, 53–56, 66–68
praise 74–75
predictions 41, 145–146
Pressley, M. 38, 41, 47–48
process 11–12, 64, 65, 148; feedback 76–78, 81, 83, 88

reactive learners 54–55
reading strategies 41, 45
reflection *see* group reflection; self-reflection
repeated practice 45, 94
responsibility, student *see* autonomy; self-monitoring
responsibility, teacher 45, 48
reviewing 39
Ryan, Richard 29

self-awareness 73–74, 88–91, 145
self-efficacy 21, 22–25, 44, 83, 90, 95, 104, 115
self-esteem 22
self-evaluation 24–25, 42, 73, 78, 92, 97, 145–146; standards 55, 106–110
self-feedback 74–75
self-monitoring 42, 67–68, 78, 87–100, 145, 148–149, 154
self-reflection 13, 73, 76, 82, 101–118, 131–133, 136; classroom activities 115–117, 146–147, 154
Self-Regulated Learner (SRLer), portrait 9–11; *see also* SRL
Self-Regulated Strategy Development program 43
Self-Regulation Empowerment Program (SREP) 59–60, 109–110, 117
self-reinforcement 41

self-standards 109–110
self-talk 41
Shute, V. J. 73
social comparisons 54
social-emotional behaviors 30
socio-contextual factors 22
SRL: focused strategies 67–68; process feedback 76, 77–78, 88; theory 7–18
Stand and Deliver 22
standardized tests *see* tests
standards 106–110
strategies 10–11, 37–50; and attribution 114–115; language of 43–44, 47, 53, 65, 93, 98–99, 136, 148; planning 54, 56; SRL 39–42, 67, 77; teaching a multi-step process 44–45, 94
stress 39, 104, 135; *see also* controllability
structured reflection time 116–117
Study Plan worksheet 67–68, 125, 127, 129
study skills 123
success interpretations 105, 107–108; *see also* tests

task analysis 54, 56, 57; teacher practices 58–61
task behaviors/process 92; *see also* self-monitoring
task components 57
task interest 21, 26–27, 95
task outcome feedback 75–76
task process feedback 76
task purpose 57
task strategies 40–41, 46, 67, 78
task structure 57
task values 25–26
teacher feedback *see* feedback, teacher
tests 60–61, 121–138
thinking, metacognition 11
thinking, patterns 103
three-phase model 12–13
time management 41
Timperley, H. 74
transitions 8
TREE strategy 41, 43, 44, 90

value 21, 22, 25, 26–28, 95

Weinstein, Claire 48
Wiliam, Dylan 79
writing skills/strategies 43–44, 47–48, 98–99

Zimmerman, Barry 12, 39, 63